Dancing in Cornmeal

Dancing in Cornmeal

Life with Autism

Nannette Beyea Silvernail

Writers Club Press
San Jose New York Lincoln Shanghai

Dancing in Cornmeal
Life with Autism

Writers Club Press
an imprint of iUniverse, Inc.

For information address:
iUniverse, Inc.
5220 S. 16th St., Suite 200
Lincoln, NE 68512
www.iuniverse.com

ISBN: 0-595-22833-X

Printed in the United States of America

For Craig and Bryn. Either of you could have written this book, if from a slightly different perspective (and with fewer words). You are two of my three greatest gifts from God.

"It was You that created me. For the wonder of myself, for the wonder of Your works, I thank You."
—Psalms 139:13-14

Contents

Part III   Little Ditties

Part IV   Recommended Reading

Preface

I'm going to try to write this preface before writing the book, just to see how accurate I end up being about the finished product. This is what I foresee:

1. A book that tells my life story as it pertains to autism. (Considering that autism affects just about every moment and every decision in my life, I foresee covering a lot of ground.)

2. A book that provides the uninformed some factual information about autism, and perhaps provides the informed a new angle to some of these facts.

3. A book that a parent can take into the bathroom or the bedroom with them, quickly read a chapter at a sitting and close the book thinking, "That's exactly what I'm going through—someone else has been there and understands."

4. A book that a friend or relative can probably read in one or two sittings, close and think, "So that's what they're going through. Now I feel like I may be able to help."

5. A little bit of inspiration.

6. A little bit more humor.

Let's see how close I come.

This book began as a bunch of essays I had written for the newsletter of our local Autism Society of America chapter. I was editor of the newsletter for about one year and took advantage of the arrangement as essayist. My pieces must have been pretty well received, as I heard nothing cruel and received requests to republish a few in other local newsletters. I remember the first day I was paid for my work. That morning, I had filled out a questionnaire. It was probably for a brand new doctor or therapist and asked a bunch of questions that didn't apply to my child's situation, such as "Name child goes by" (at the time, she didn't go, come, or look at you in response to any name) or "First Word." I felt I had to qualify my answer of "ma ma" because she hadn't said it or much else in a few years.

I came to the "Mother's Occupation" space. "Homemaker, House-keeper, Mother, At-home Teacher, Unlicensed Therapist" all applied, but my passion was for writing. I sat in my friend's kitchen that after-noon and told her, "I wanted so much to put "Writer," but I'm really not a writer until I've been paid for my work." She left the room for a minute and came back with something in her hand.

"Remember that article you gave me to read the other day?" she asked. "Yeah," I answered. "I loved it," she said, then opened her hand to reveal a quarter and held it out to me. "Thanks."

I took the quarter, put it in my pocket and I've been filling in that blank with "Writer" ever since.

I hope you think what's contained in these pages is worth more than a quarter, particularly if you're the one who shelled out the list price for it. I hope even more that you have a friend in your life as smart and caring as my friend.

This book is not a story about a child who was cured of autism. Lauren has made gains over the years, but she is far from living a life resembling that of an ordinary child. Despite my having no great discovery to share, I feel led to write this book because of what I do have to share—years of pursuing autism education and discovering what works best for Lauren, and for our whole family. If you're involved with a child with autism, perhaps reading this book early on in the diagnosis will give you a jump on some lessons that took our family a few years to learn.

Before this book, I had never written a complete account of our family's introduction to the world of autism. These chapters had to be written from scratch, which made me thankful for my journals, though I wish I had written in them more frequently. (Most journal entries, which I addressed directly to Lauren or Bryn, depending on whose journal it was, began something like this: "I'm sorry I haven't written here in so long, but my excuse is a good one. I've spent every waking hour being the best mom I know how to you and your sister." I don't know if I wrote that so that my daughters would someday forgive me for the limited accounts, or so that I would remember to forgive myself.)

The second section contains many stories from my life with autism, but its purpose is to convey some of the most important lessons I've learned since my adventures with autism began. I imagine future years will continue to teach me and change me, but I'm hopeful the new lessons will detail and enhance, never contradict, the lessons I share here.

In the third section of the book, there is something extra. These are what I call my "little ditties"—thoughts that were in my head that wouldn't let me sleep until I let them out. These were the essays that started my writing career and the reason that I wanted to reach a wider audience. I don't think it's that important that you know me or my children or our story. But I do think it's important that I share those thoughts that seemed desperate for life. Perhaps they were meant for someone other than me.

Before continuing, I want to address my use of pronouns throughout the book. When it's cumbersome to speak generically of a child with autism as "he or she," I choose the pronoun "she." There are actually more males with autism than females (the ratio is 3:1) but most of my experience and writing is about a girl with autism, so I stick with the feminine pronouns for consistency. To compensate for this choice, I use masculine pronouns when I'm speaking nonspecifically about an individual who doesn't have autism.

Thanks for giving the words before you some of your time. I know how precious each moment is in a life challenged by autism in whatever capacity. I hope your future moments are blessed in some way, big or small, for the moments spent here.

Thanks

This book was many years in the making; not many years in the writing, but many years in the living and experiencing to have the stories and words to share with you today. Even when I was sure I could pull it off, the goal-setting required of a writer wasn't part of the picture until a great number of people suddenly took the time to send me notes and e-mails which echoed the sentiment of my favorite fan and husband: You can do it.

Sheila Tremper and Elena Makievsky, your confidence in me was like the Little Engine mantra whispered into my ear even late at night at this keyboard. Both of these ladies have experience as moms of a child with a disability, are creative and talented in their respective fields, and have my utmost respect. Your insistence that I had all I needed but a self-imposed deadline was the greatest gift either of you could ever have given me. I'm proud to call you friends.

Vicki Clarke and Marian Joiner are two more women I've been proud to call friends, though our friendships began in professional relationships. These women have been the most knowledgeable, compassionate, intuitive and hard-working therapists Lauren will ever know. Much of what I've learned over the years, I have learned (or had affirmed) by one of these ladies. I can't imagine having gotten through the toughest moments without having Marian or Vicki around. Each of these ladies has years of training and hands-on experience, which might explain their amazing ability to assess the true problems behind a child's severe communication disorder, while also knowing how to address it on a day to day basis. But their innate ability to sense the intelligence and spirit in a silent and frightened child has nothing to do with education or experience. It is, and has been, a gift from Heaven.

Thank you, DeLee Eden, Diana Toso, Jackie Verner and a few other homeschooling moms in the wings. You're dear friends and faithful praying partners who have a knack for keeping me spiritually afloat with words of encouragement just as a big wave is rolling in.

To be purposely redundant, Craig and Bryn, my husband and older daughter, are my greatest fans and my beloved cohorts in crime. If they hadn't insisted, "Sit, write, we'll be fine" hundreds of times, this book wouldn't exist. (Craig took two whole weeks off from his job to care for the children, which allowed me to finish this book during normal daylight hours! Most of my writing takes place on weekends and during those normally wasted hours between midnight and 6:00 A.M.) Of course, without my younger daughter, my precious Lauren, who forces me to seek God's wisdom rather than my own about twenty times a day, there wouldn't be much of a story either. Thank you, family.

Thanks, also, Dad and Mom. Dad loved that I was an A student while growing up, that I am now a writer and that we can have terrific instant messenger conversations on the internet. My mom has loved me even when I wasn't getting A's in school, will love me even if I'm suddenly unable to write my own name, and always tells me what a gift it is to know me. Who could ask for more?

PART I
Lauren's Story

o o o o o o o o o o o o o o o o o o o o o o o o o o o o o o o o

He drew a circle that shut me out—
Heretic, rebel, a thing to flout.
But love and I had the wit to win:
We drew a circle that took him in.

——*Outwitted by Edwin Markham*

How It All Began

It was a Spring weekend in upstate New York. Our fifteen-month-old daughter, Bryn, was happily riding in the back seat of the car. My husband, Craig, was driving, and I sat in the passenger seat as we made our way to my parents' house for a little family reunion. I don't know why, but the two hour drive between our house and my parents' was always beautiful. I don't recall a trip that wasn't sunny with the bluest of skies, particularly when we drove beside the Neversink reservoir. We passed through miles of woods, then it opened up on one side to the man-made reservoir. It was during these miles that I said to Craig, "You know, there's the slightest chance that I might be pregnant."

I loved telling Craig such things. There are so few things with which you can so quickly and easily impact your husband's emotions. I've only done it twice, but it was fun both times. My body works like a clock and, though I was only one day late, I had been pregnant before. There weren't any other definite signs, I just *felt* pregnant.

"But, we didn't..." he started to say.

"Oh, yes, we did," I corrected him. "I've been thinking over the past two weeks that I may have miscounted."

"Wow," he said. We agreed that if there were no changes by Monday, I'd buy a home pregnancy test. Of course, I was visiting my mom, so I couldn't resist telling her and she bought the pregnancy test for me. It turned out to be fun watching the drugstore clerk get a price check on the particular box Mom placed on the counter. The cashier was obviously wondering if the test was for this probably post-menopausal woman.

Over the weekend, my dad grilled a variety of meats and I couldn't eat enough. I felt ravenous, and at one point, both Craig and Mom looked at my plate, rolled their eyes and laughed. Craig decided he'd seen this behavior once before and took action. My dad is known to like his hamburger mooing and his grilled chicken clucking, but we had always just laughed about it and eaten around anything too raw for our tastes. This day, Craig cut open each piece of meat before I ate it and boldly threw any suspect pieces back on the grill, telling Dad he preferred it well done.

On Monday, the pregnancy test was positive and the entire pregnancy was as carefully tended as that first weekend when we only suspected. On exactly the first day after the first trimester, my morning sickness abated. I remember the day well, as it was also the day we moved into a house in Pennsylvania. I had delivered my first baby on her due date, and this time, again, I delivered a baby girl on her due date. We arrived at the birthing center in the pushing stage. The mid-wife walked in a few minutes after we did and said, "OK, you're all ready. You can push." About an hour later, Lauren Therese was born. The umbilical cord was wrapped around her neck for a moment, but the mid-wife and nurse worked fast. Her first Apgar score was 8 and her second was 10, just like my first baby. My first baby, however, was born in a hospital and experienced a few more complications. My first delivery had been excruciatingly painful, making this one seem like a walk in the park by comparison. I went home six hours after delivery and happily woke up to give Lauren her feedings in the middle of the night. I couldn't even get up to give Bryn her feedings her first week home.

Relatively, Lauren's birth was easy on me and seemed to yield a perfectly healthy baby. Over the years, moms of children with autism have asked me, "Did you have a C section, too?" I guess in hopes of validating their suspicions over what caused their child's autism. But I can honestly say that there was nothing about Lauren's birth upon which I could possibly place blame. Both my mid-wife and Lauren's doctor made trips out to our home on her first and second days to check her. She was a little yellow with jaundice, but a few hours on my bed in the sunlight coming through a big bay window pinked her right up. (It was winter, so we turned the upstairs thermostat to 80, stripped the baby, then my mom and I took turns sitting half dressed next to her.)

During Lauren's first check-up at the doctor's office at one-week-old, the doctor made one memorable comment. After thoroughly looking Lauren over while speaking to her in a quiet "baby" tone, he turned to me all business and announced, "She's a keeper!" To this day, while playing and cuddling with her, Craig, Bryn or I are often heard saying, "Dr. Moeser was right, Lauren. You're a keeper!"

◆   ◆   ◆

Now I'm going to jump ahead nine years—to today. This chapter has been very hard to write because for most of the last three months, Lauren has been a very difficult child. She has been uninterested in anything but seeking sensory input (stimming)[1] and she has frequent outbursts of anger or very sad crying. When she is angry or upset, she hits or bites herself or others. When we leave her alone to calm down, she continues to be aggressive and particularly to bite herself. She doesn't lack nerve endings. She has bruises where she has bitten herself and she avoids those areas. This tells me how severe the pain is that is causing her outbursts. If she seeks the pain of biting herself to somehow diminish the agony of what precipitates her outbursts, that agony must be unbearable. Certainly no form of physical punishment is going to speak to her about her behavior. Have you ever been bitten? That's the worst kind of physical punishment.

At one point, Lauren had worked her way up her arm and began biting her shoulder. We can't get near her when she's like this, as she hurts us, and our attempts at intervention have consistently proven only to escalate the violence. We've removed all hard surfaces from her bedroom, except the frame of her bed, and this is her place to go or to be placed when she's out of control. Sometimes we have to lock the door for a few minutes to keep her in there until she's calm enough to come out. But most of the time, she willingly throws herself on her bed and doesn't try to come out until she's calm. I believe she doesn't want to hurt us, or to have us see her this way. She wants every opportunity to calm down as well.

After about two months of this behavior, Craig and I decided we had to rule out a physiological cause. Though she had no symptoms of illness, we took her to her pediatrician and asked for all orifices to be checked out for anything that might be causing pain. Lauren's usual doctor wasn't in and a young doctor newer to the practice came into the examining room. I knew from having seen this doctor with Bryn that this man was a kind and thorough doctor. I felt bad for him, knowing what he had in store with Lauren. Lauren is terribly frightened of doctors' offices, or any place that resembles a doctor's office with a waiting room and a mysterious hall with little rooms leading from it. I'm sure the unpleasantness she suffered as a young child being tested for UTI[2] difficulties, then for her autism diagnosis, did nothing to squelch any fears of this environment. Lately, with every trip to the pediatrician and dentist, her anxiety has grown. This particular visit, despite our reassurances all the way there, as soon as we drove into the familiar parking lot, Lauren began sobbing. In the waiting room, she made a soft, high-pitched whine over and over again as her body shook with fear. She reminded me of a wounded animal, wanting help but fearful of the help walking toward her—sure that this will only lead to her complete destruction. Every time people opened the door to the hallway to the examining rooms, Lauren jumped up and quickly closed it behind them, her last bid at separating herself from the long walk to the "torture chambers."

I'm sure the doctor had heard the intermittent sobs and our struggle with Lauren in the waiting room, then in the hall to the examining room, then in the examining room. I was so proud of him when he quickly figured out that no attempts at calming would help. *Get in and out as quickly as possible* was the only strategy for this situation. Craig held Lauren in his lap. I held her arms and attempted to block her legs while the doctor quickly used his various scopes and a tongue depressor, then took a swab to her throat. (I don't remember how many tongue depressors she broke with her teeth trying to keep him out.) Lauren received a clean bill of health from the visual check. We waited what seemed like a very long time for results to a strep test. Lauren paced the room sobbing. The doctor finally came in and told us the strep test was positive. "Hooray!" Craig and I said in unison, then laughed and explained that we're just so happy to have something to treat.

"But," the doctor said slowly, with eyes wide, "you'll have to give her an antibiotic...we have a one time shot I could give..." I smiled as I told him that she took liquid antibiotics just fine. I'm sure the doctor couldn't imagine us ever getting that mouth open again without a professional and some vise grips. It made me realize that Lauren's doctors have never seen her calm, cooperative and communicative (beyond communicating very well that she wants to leave). I knew short-term high dose antibiotics made Lauren's sensory system go haywire. I think the only time we had ever seen self-abusive behavior before was when she was on the first day of a three-day antibiotic, which we immediately traded in for a lower dosage one. I reassured the doctor that Lauren was a different child outside the doctor's office and that she was accustomed to taking medicines and supplements with no problem. He just slowly nodded in disbelief. Later that night, along with my prayers for Lauren, I threw in one for the doctor—that today's experience not frighten him into a different career.

Lauren's behavior was different but still aggressive while she was on the antibiotic for ten days. From previous experience, we assumed it would be. The day after she went off the antibiotic, we went outside for one of the first times after a cold winter. Lauren suddenly started crying and acting angry and we didn't know why. Craig took her into the house while Bryn and I went to some appointment in the car.

When we returned, Craig said, "Well, I know why Lauren was so upset. I gave her a bath when she came in and bumps started appearing all over her arms and back. She must have gotten into a nest of fire ants!" Anyone who lives in the Southeastern United States appreciates the horrific sensation of even one fire ant bite. We had never seen an ant on her, but Lauren had about a dozen bites on her arms, back and stomach. The year before, she had one on her foot that grew to be a blister the size of a large jelly bean. She couldn't put a shoe on that foot for two weeks. So, Lauren's *I'm hurting and angry* behavior continued for another two weeks and we continued to explain it away with the ant bites.

When the ant bites healed and the behavior continued, our family didn't know what to do but pray. In between the opportunities to practice self-defense and our heartbreak, we prayed and we asked friends to pray. We also looked for answers. Another strep test showed the strep was gone. I began looking at what other changes may have been made without our realizing it.

Lauren had been on a high dose acidophilus (healthy flora—an anti-yeast supplement) for about a year. I remembered that her last bout of very poor behavior occurred before she went on this supplement. We had seen huge improvements immediately after she began taking it. I knew when Lauren started on her antibiotic that antibiotics kill healthy flora. However, I thought that Lauren's supplement dosage would be enough to counter the attack. I also realized the timing of another dietary change we had made: Craig had found a bread that Lauren would eat at about the same time she started on the antibiotic. (Lauren is gluten-free so finding a gluten-free bread that makes tolerable peanut butter and jelly on toast—her favorite—seemed like a miracle.) In other words, after a long time without yeast, we had introduced a yeast bread to Lauren's diet (which she ate for as many meals as we would allow) as well as jelly (a sugar which converts to yeast in the body) while she was also taking an antibiotic. All of these things contributed to an excess of unhealthy flora (yeast) in her digestive tract and we hadn't increased her dosage of healthy flora to counter it and keep her system balanced. Now, I'm no nutritionist or chemist, but I felt sure this barrage of unhealthy flora on Lauren's system couldn't be good. I tripled her supplement dosage and told Craig, "No more bread or jelly. It's back to the gluten-free rice crackers until we find a decent yeast-free bread!" (Craig is often the parent in charge of Lauren's breakfast and PB&J on toast had quickly become an easy favorite so this was very sad news to him.)[3]

Within about three days, we had our sweet child back. The first morning Lauren woke up, came into our bedroom and giggled as she tried to kiss us awake, I rejoiced! For too many mornings, Craig and I had been awakened by someone throwing a fit or hitting us awake. After her morning bath, she sat in a chair and peacefully looked at a picture book, slowly turning the pages, smiling and touching favorite pictures. She hadn't even been able to sit still for months, and if I'd handed her a book, she would have thrown it at me. I brought a puzzle to the table at snack time, talked about the pieces and asked her to help me put them back in, first one piece at a time, then two. She put all the pieces in before finishing her snack, then left the table with the puzzle and continued to take the pieces out and put them back in. I hadn't gotten anything this close to academics near her in months! Of course not, I hadn't been able to get myself close to her in months—certainly not without fear of being suddenly slapped or kicked. Thank you, God! Yes, I made some fumbling changes to her diet in hopes of hitting on something, but I never feel sure that what I'm doing is *the* answer. I feel like we're back at a plateau—a new starting point of possibility and hope. I just thank God for this and keep praying.

The rest of this book tells more of the story of Lauren and our family between the time of her diagnosis and this latest, difficult time we seem to have overcome for now.

At this moment of my writing, Lauren is nine years old. As you can see, she is not cured of autism. Though we hear some word approximations every day and we have heard a few phrases come out of Lauren as clear as a bell, I don't yet consider Lauren a verbal child. I praise her and thank God with her every night for the words that she said and that her family understood that day. Lauren seems happy that I appreciate her efforts and that I recognize that we are part of the effort at understanding her, too. But Lauren primarily uses photos, pictures and gestures to communicate clearly. Lauren has said the word "cookie" very clearly in the past. However, if I hold a cookie outside her reach and require her to say the word to receive the cookie, she will try every other form of communication that has worked for her in the past to indicate that she wants a cookie. She'll then try new forms of communication. (She's usually quite resourceful.) But she may spend the rest of the day sobbing for lack of a cookie before she will produce any sound resembling "cookie." Lauren's speech therapist tells me the word for this is apraxia. She's not being defiant. She's not playing me for the fool. After all, she's not a fool. If she could get the word out for something she wants, she certainly wouldn't go without and search for whatever very difficult means she can find to communicate to her mom, "I want this." Her communicative pleas are quite understandable. She's often saying, "I want you so much to understand me. Why don't you understand me? Do you understand me and are just saying 'no' to my needs?"

One day when I was probably questioning every choice I'd ever made for Lauren because she wasn't speaking yet, I remember her speech therapist kindly hushing me. "Nannette," she said, "Lauren will speak when she is ready to speak. We're doing everything we can to encourage it, but she has to get to that point. That's not something you can do for her." One of my favorite speakers on autism, Diane Twachtman, says something else that reassures me. She talks about children with autism having the same desire to fit in and to be as independent as possible as any other child in the classroom or on the playground. What motivation would any person have for not wanting these things? I see how Lauren imitates her family and friends like any other child learning a skill. She copies the way I "love on" our cats. She copies her friends, trying to wrap a sash around herself the way they do when playing dress-up. She copies the way we each use a fork to eat. She smiles and relishes the praise when she masters any of these things. I see how she loves simply spending time with her family more than anything in the world. I see how she imitates our sounds and turn-takes in "conversation" though we don't understand her end of it. She obviously wants to join in what we all have going here. When she exhibits the desires of a typical child, how can I presume these desires stop when it comes to speech? She undoubtedly wants to be able to speak like all those she loves and admires. It's so difficult for her simply because of whatever damage to her body or brain was caused by this thing called autism.

The rest of this book is about the difficulties, and the effects they have on a family. It's about what we've tried and what's helped and what hasn't. It's also about our joy and what we have learned—the intangibles that have probably most helped us get through the toughest moments in this life with autism.

The Four Questions

It's always awkward telling someone for the first time that Lauren has autism. I commonly don't know if the person already has a clue about her disability or if this will take them completely by surprise and make them feel awkward. As Lauren grows older, I think her autism is more apparent to on-lookers. However, I'm with her most of the time and have grown accustomed to her behavior and mannerisms, so I'm not too sure which ones make her look different. I also see more and more ill-behaved and hyperactive children whose behavior makes me think Lauren's isn't so unusual. But most of these children can answer the question, "How old are you?" or "What's your name?" And that seems to be the big giveaway. That's when I feel forced to say something to make up for her silence.

"She has autism and doesn't have much speech yet," I usually say, "but she's nine years old." It rolls off my tongue like a name, rank and serial number. After my revelation, I'm inevitably asked one of four questions:

1. *What's autism?*

2. *How did you know she had autism?*

3. *What causes autism?*

4. *What's her prognosis?* (Or some form of this, such as, *"Will she get better?"*)

This is one reason I wrote this book. I'm just tired of answering these questions. I always feel that in the limited amount of time I have to answer (as Lauren is trying to run away or grab something off a store shelf, etc.) I don't do the answer justice. For once, I'm going to sit down, take the time to think out my answers, and include them in this book. Then next time and forevermore, when Lauren is dragging me away as I'm asked a huge question, I can give the inquiring person the opportunity for a complete answer in way of a book title. (Or when I'm asked one of these questions at a party. My hosts must also be tired of me reverting to this topic in every conversation. But when you have a child who finds a comfortable place in a new social situation, then won't leave it, that can inspire some inquiring minds. Especially if the comfortable place is under a table or in the middle of a small, busy stairway.)

In answer to the first question:

What is Autism?

Autism is a neurological disorder that becomes apparent during early childhood. There is no medical test for autism.[4] A diagnosis is made by parent and professional observation. If the child's symptoms fall within the officially accepted criteria for autism, then a diagnosis of autism is given.[5] Clusters of criteria fall under three categories:

1. communication (verbal and non-verbal)

2. social interaction

3. atypical behavior

Lists of possible symptoms of autism are found in literature and web sites from many autism organizations, such as the Autism Research Institute (ARI) and the Autism Society of America (ASA). However, no list of autism symptoms is exhaustive. One child with autism may possess little or no speech, while another talks non-stop on select topics. Some people with autism have many behaviors that seem bizarre, such as hand flapping, spinning or moaning. Others are hardly noticeable in a crowd. Some adults with autism are married and hold jobs that require frequent interaction and problem solving. Others never live independently.

Autism is an umbrella diagnosis. This is what makes it so confusing. It is a label for a mix and match of a variety of observable symptoms. My daughter is non-verbal and has the diagnosis of autism. I know many children who speak and are in regular education classrooms who also have the diagnosis of autism. This leads to many problems:

1. Parents whose children are not speaking are often questioned by well-meaning people who say, "I know this little boy who is talking really well. Maybe you should talk to his parents and see what they did for him." Usually, a child is non-verbal through no parental neglect in treatment. There just happens to be a broad range of levels within this diagnosis.

2. Parents seeking support at an autism support group may only find discouragement. I attended a support group for the first time years ago and remember listening to a father and mother go on and on about their fear that their son may be ambidextrous. Their greatest concern at the moment was that he wrote equally well with both hands. The boy was speaking and at grade level in most of his regular ed. class activities. I was on the verge of exploding before they stopped talking. If only my daughter, who was older than their son, would say a word or pick up a crayon! When I realized that most of the parents at the meeting had speaking children who were functioning at levels much higher than my daughter, I didn't feel much camaraderie with these people.

3. Some programs claim to have cures for children with autism, but fail to mention that their success rate was measured using children who began the program at high functioning levels. Any two or three-year-old with autism who is speaking to any extent has a very good chance of drastic improvement in any reputable program. I was so glad when I heard Tony Attwood, a Clinical Psychologist

specializing in autism, say at a conference that no child should be thought to have a firm diagnosis of autism until he or she is over six years old. Any child under six who improves so dramatically that people claim he or she was "cured" of autism probably should not have had the diagnosis of autism.

There are many people, including myself, who believe that there should be great effort put forth to distinguish the various forms of autism. This would give parents a better understanding of the type of "autism" that affects their child and would give researchers, doctors and therapists better understanding of how to pinpoint research and treatment.

In an attempt to better address the broad range of autism symptoms and severity, the diagnosis of Pervasive Developmental Delay (PDD)[6] was added to the DSM at about the time Lauren was diagnosed. Children who did not fit the severest description of autism began receiving this diagnosis instead of autism. As our pediatric neurologist said, "It just means that we have no idea what this child's future brings or how severe the disorder will be for her." Unfortunately, some diagnosticians must have presented this diagnosis as something very different from autism. I have met a few parents who didn't know where to go to seek help because their children were diagnosed with PDD, so they didn't think their child had autism. Many informational and support groups did start including PDD alongside the word autism, but I still encounter parents who insist that "My child isn't autistic. She has PDD." That's as accurate as saying "This shape isn't a rectangle. It's a square!" (Squares are one type of rectangle.)

An official list of criteria can't describe all the many ways that autism may affect a person's abilities and behavior. Throughout this book, I tell many stories to help you understand my family's experience with autism. However, the way that autism affects my daughter may be very different from how it affects a person with autism whom you know. It's obvious that autism is an umbrella diagnosis when you observe a classroom or group of people with autism. But I am also reminded just by observing and working with one child that it is an umbrella encompassing many other umbrellas. I see symptoms of obsessive/compulsive disorder (OCD), Tourette's Syndrome, ADD, ADHD and dyslexia in one small child at my house every day. These aren't just the imaginings of a mom who minored in psychology in college. I have successfully employed many strategies encountered in books and web sites addressing these other diagnoses, not autism. Craig and I sometimes joke that his dyslexia and my OCD just happened to make up the perfect genetic mix for Lauren's autism. He completely understands her inability to visually track and I completely understand her extreme need for order. It may just be a private joke, but I think we're a step ahead of anything that the medical community will accept and agree upon in writing any time soon.

There are many people walking on the earth who possess some qualities of autism, but no diagnosis. I often wonder at the decision-making that went into deciding when these symptoms qualify as a disorder. At what point are a person's symptoms not just part of his personality, but a disorder to be overcome? I gave this much thought while writing this today. Craig and I have had many discouraging moments with Lauren this week. Despite some gains being made, Lauren has begun biting and hitting herself from time to time, which she hadn't done in weeks. Of course we're always concerned for her safety and health, but this time, it seems as though we're angry with each other, and much sadder about the whole situation. A feeling of hopelessness is setting in.

I read portions of Donna Williams's book, *Autism: An Inside-Out Approach*, to find answers to Lauren's self-abusive behavior. Donna Williams[7] has taught me more about my daughter than any "expert" I've ever consulted. Just reading a few bits and pieces, I am reminded that autism is a big part of who Lauren is. Lately, we've been seeing the autism as the enemy, hoping that there are only one or two battles left to fight before it is vanquished. Donna Williams's words suggest to me that Lauren will grow and change in tune with, and in spite of, her autism, just as any child will grow and change as he or she approaches adulthood, despite obstacles, and because of obstacles. But is this reason to breathe a sigh of relief? Lauren is still hurting herself and when anyone I love is hurting, I'm ready to go to battle for him or her.

This is one of those moments when I must separate the mom-self from the therapist-self to understand our situation. My therapist/theorist-self can easily see the bigger picture—that Lauren has made steady gains over the years in her ability to communicate and interact and that she will likely continue in this pattern. But my mom-self knows that as she grows larger, even if tantrums and aggressive episodes are fewer and farther between, it is becoming more and more difficult to get through them now that our daughter weighs over one hundred pounds and grows stronger each day. She is also not using the toilet independently and tends to rip at her clothes and fight to keep them off when she's having a difficult time. It's not the autism that is the enemy. It's time. Puberty is just around the corner. How will Craig and I continue to care for our daughter if she has not overcome some of these problems by the time menses hits? This is why we have a pass/fail mentality lately. The only vision we have of our future if we "fail" to slay this monster that haunts her is very grim. I will love my precious child, autism and all, unconditionally until the day I die. But it may kill me sooner, rather than later, to see her and her family enduring the future we fear.

Time truly is the greater enemy. When Lauren was much younger, Craig and I were discussing the progress she had made and the various stages she had gone through, seemingly due in no part to any intervention or program we had undertaken. "I think autism is self-curing," I said. "I think if given three hundred years, Lauren would have enough time to make all the adjustments she needs to make to adapt her brain and body to the demands of our world and the people in it." I still believe this. There's been no trick to Lauren's slow but steady progress over the years. When we suspect that something is a problem for her, we make the adjustments needed, whether in the environment or in her diet. Lauren does this all the time, too. By closing all the doors to a room, turning all the lights on and off, seeking pressure or keeping a blanket over her head, she's accommodating her brain's and body's differences. When a troubling behavior is suddenly no longer troubling her (or us), we could say that we successfully brought her out of it. But the fact is that this child with autism got herself through it. She's slowly but surely "curing" herself of this autism with the help of some very committed associates—her family, friends and therapists.

The big problem is that we only have about sixty to eighty years on this earth. Lauren's committed associates would like her to spend most of those years with the ability to express her needs, her wishes and her dreams. We want her to know the joy of relationships—the ins and outs and ups and downs of getting along with strangers, friends and family. We want the possibility to exist for a loving married relationship in her future. We want her to know God. And I want her to tell me all she knows about God.

That's why the autism that affects Lauren is a disorder. The day she can have all the things I just mentioned, autism will be just an imperfect descriptor of some personality traits. But today, autism is standing in the way of relationships, dreams and opportunity; and sometimes it seems to cause her pain. So today, autism is the enemy.

"How Did You Know...?"

Lauren was officially diagnosed with autism when she was twenty months old. Craig and I were told by many professionals who saw her that we were fortunate to receive a diagnosis so early, as early intervention had proven to be very important in helping many children with autism. Ironically, if we had left it up to the medical community to catch Lauren's autism, her diagnosis would have been much later in coming.

Lauren's first year seemed normal in just about every way. She rolled over, sat up, crawled and walked on schedule. She was very interactive with her family, particularly laughing at all her sister's antics. She was a peaceful, easy-going baby. Considering her sister had been much more demanding and kept me up many nights her first year, I felt quite blessed with my second daughter.

When Lauren was about one year old, my suspicions that there was something different about her became a little bit of a concern. I was sure that Bryn was consistently saying "Mama" by her first birthday, but Lauren had never said "Mama" and had perhaps blurted out a "Dada" only once. For a month or two, she had been saying something resembling "So Big!" each time we asked her how big she was. We'd help her throw her hands in the air and she would giggle and wiggle with glee at the game. But on her first birthday, I realized that we weren't getting that out of her anymore, either.

Lauren also had some odd habits that I couldn't ignore. She sometimes stared off into space and was completely unresponsive to anyone around her. While so absorbed in her own little world, sometimes her body would suddenly become tense and she would slightly shake all over. This frightened me and I often tickled or shook her until she came out of her bizarre stupor.

At Lauren's one year checkup with the pediatrician, I mentioned my concerns to the doctor. I told her Lauren wasn't talking yet. The doctor told me not to worry about it because children mature at different rates. We were in the doctor's office frequently at that time because Lauren had many ear infections and had to return for an ear check every time she finished a round of antibiotics. At every visit, I would mention her lack of talking, but this particular practice had six doctors and I saw a different one each time. Each doctor brushed off my concerns and told me to bring it up at her eighteen-month appointment if it was still a concern.

When Lauren was fifteen months old, I was babysitting a friend's twelve-month-old daughter. Before leaving one afternoon, my friend told her daughter to show me what she could do. Her mom said, "Where's your nose?" and this baby carefully pointed to her nose. Mom asked "Where's your ear?" and this little girl pointed to her ear. This continued right to the belly button and I was legitimately impressed. I knew that my Lauren couldn't point to any body part. I felt guilty. I had failed her as a mother! Despite the fact that I was a full-time mom, I thought that I must have somehow not taught Lauren something that I had taught Bryn. I laid her on the changing table after her bath that evening and said, "Where's your nose?" She looked away from me. I used my most sing-songy voice to get her attention and said, "Lauren, show Mommy your nose." She looked away again. After many more tries, I declared (I don't remember if it was only to myself or aloud), "How do you teach someone who won't look at you?!" I didn't know at that moment how central to my life that question would become. I still fight this battle.

Finally, at one of Lauren's sick visits, I again mentioned my concerns, perhaps more emphatically than before, to one of the pediatricians I had not seen in a few months. I told her how Lauren wasn't talking or even pointing, and how I couldn't get her attention. I didn't say at the time that she didn't seem to hear me, because I knew that Lauren could hear a few quiet sounds from across the house, such as the click of the television being turned on and the sound of water running into the bathtub. (Lauren loved to watch children's videos and to take baths.) This doctor was concerned and gave me the name of an Ear, Nose and Throat specialist (ENT) that I should call to have Lauren's hearing tested.

The first time I heard the word autism used in conjunction with Lauren was in a conversation with my mother. I had always shared my concerns about Lauren with my mom and she had spoken to a friend of the family whose degree was in psychology. My mom had told this friend about some of Lauren's delays and interesting behavior, then asked, "Does this sound anything like autism to you?" The friend admitted to not having studied much about autism in school, but that it did sound like a possibility. Lauren's ENT was the second person to say that word, "autism."

I took Lauren into the ENT's office for a hearing test. It was a traditional hearing test, in a soundproof booth, with a bear or clown toy with cymbals in one corner and a different electrical noise-making toy in the opposite corner. I sat with seventeen-month-old Lauren in my lap facing a window where a technician sat on the other side. There were speakers in the booth and this woman directed me and spoke to Lauren over a microphone.

The first time one of the toys was activated, Lauren stiffened up and turned slightly in the opposite direction. I knew my child. I knew that this sound startled her and that her frightened reaction was a response to her hearing the sound. The technician activated the other toy and Lauren stiffened and actively avoided looking in that direction as well. The woman called Lauren's name over the speakers and Lauren stiffened and looked down, not up as she was being told. I knew Lauren heard every sound I heard in that booth and that this was a very unpleasant experience for her. I wanted to say, "She heard that! Didn't you see her stiffen?" But I was quiet, as I didn't want to somehow taint the test results.

After the test, the doctor told me that Lauren's hearing tested very poorly, but that could be at least partially from fluid that was still in her middle ear. She recommended surgery to put ear tubes in Lauren's ears to allow the fluid to drain, then we would test her hearing again; only this time with a Brainstem Evoked Response, or BER, which would not require Lauren's cooperation.

I know many young children undergo ear tube surgery, but that experience is burned into my memory. A body that small being anesthetized is so limp and lifeless, it's frightening. Though the surgery lasted only about ten minutes, I could not have imagined how distraught I could become in ten minutes. When Lauren was wheeled into her recovery cubicle, I cried. Her body was laid on an adult sized bed pillow. I had never seen her on a pillow and it made her look even smaller and more lifeless. I sat close and listened for her breath while I waited for her to wake up. By the time we arrived home, Lauren seemed as active and happy as usual. She recuperated fine and her ear fluid finally drained.

The day of the BER, Lauren was given a sedative, then I nursed her to sleep. She lay in my lap as electrodes were stuck to her head. The technician typed things into a keyboard, which sent sound waves to Lauren's brain. We could instantly see lines on a monitor which represented Lauren's brain immediately responding to the various sound waves. This test showed us that Lauren's hearing was fine.

After this hearing test, Lauren's ENT told me she would send her report to Lauren's pediatrician. I asked the doctor if she thought further testing was needed. She said yes. I asked her if she thought Lauren might have autism. She told me that she saw many children like Lauren and autism was definitely a possibility. Lauren's pediatrician called me when she received the hearing test results. She wanted to have Lauren start speech therapy. I told her that I first wanted a consultation with her, that she might thoroughly observe Lauren. I mentioned some other delays and behaviors that we were seeing in Lauren that I hadn't mentioned before. The doctor agreed and we met at lunch time one day in her office.

Today, as I look back at that paramount visit with Lauren's pediatrician, the most bizarre aspect to it is that Craig wasn't with me. I think that at the time, I thought the doctor would only recommend further testing. I remember thinking that there would probably soon be many appointments Craig would need to attend, so I didn't want to take him from work any more than necessary. In every other respect, however, I was very prepared. Upon walking into the doctor's office, I handed her a six page typed report listing all of Lauren's developmental delays and (as yet) unexplainable behaviors. I tried to create a thorough picture of Lauren so that the doctor would be as successful as possible at discerning her needs. It's a good thing I brought the report, as the only activities Lauren engaged in during that hour and a half were playing with a doorstop and with the window blinds. (Though these two activities probably spoke volumes to the doctor.)

Before the doctor even finished reading the last page, she piled the papers back together and slowly said to me, "Your daughter has all the classical signs of autism." She flipped through the pages again to point out some specifically telling descriptions, then mentioned that her behavior in the office was symptomatic as well. At one point, she stopped and pushed a box of Kleenex toward me. "Go ahead and cry," she said. I think her own emotions about having to give me the news were overwhelming her, as I felt fine. My biggest worry was that I wouldn't remember word for word everything that the doctor told me so that I could repeat it all to Craig that evening. I kept thinking, "Well, finally we have an answer. All we need is an accurate diagnosis, then we can gather information and do whatever we have to do to help our baby." My, but how naive I was…

To rule out other possible diagnoses, the pediatrician ordered a blood work up and an MRI[8] for Lauren. I remember both experiences vividly, as all parents do when they must submit a child to pain and fear "for her own good." I remember being told it might be easier if I didn't stay in the room with her. My response was, "I have a lot of experience holding her down," which I guess convinced the medical personnel that I wasn't going to cry, faint or fawn. (When Lauren was eleven months old, I had insisted that I would hold her during tests she needed to rule out any serious cause for her urinary tract infections. So, I wasn't lying when I said I had experience holding her down. But it is possible to be firm, helpful, reassuring, and to cry all at the same time.)

To put her to sleep for the MRI (as she needed to lie perfectly still in a tube) Lauren was given a sedative through an IV while I held her in my arms. Her arm was taped to a board so that she wouldn't pull the needle out of her arm when she moved. But each time Lauren started to fall asleep, she pulled her arms up as all babies do, whacked herself in the head with the board and startled awake! Craig finally took over holding her because he had a special way of putting her to sleep while standing and swaying her back and forth in front of him. (The board was beneath her in this position.) The nurses or technicians responsible for sedating her were amazed at how high a dosage was necessary. I will always wonder whether so much sedative in such a small body further harmed Lauren's brain. The pediatric neurologist who later told us all of Lauren's test results were normal also told us that he wouldn't have expected anything else and that, years ago, he stopped ordering these tests on children like Lauren.

The pediatrician sent us to the pediatric neurologist to confirm Lauren's diagnosis and to give us whatever else his expertise had to offer. This doctor was new to an established pediatric neurologist's practice. The original doctor in the practice was unavailable for months. We believed the new doctor wouldn't have been hired if he wasn't qualified, so we went to this man. He confirmed the diagnosis, but had little else to offer. He was unfamiliar with any local programs or organizations other than the local parent support group network for families with children of any disability. He gave us no information on the variety of existing theories and therapies that were available across America. (The internet wasn't even in my home yet.) However, Craig and I liked this man. He seemed to sincerely like Lauren, and he gave us the most valuable piece of advice we've received from anyone on this journey so far. He said, "From this point forward, there will be a lot of stupid people telling you what you should do for your daughter, including myself! Just remember that you know your child better than anyone else and you are the only ones who know what's best for her." This doctor earned our utmost respect for those lines, which we have remembered in every encounter with a new "expert."

What Causes Autism?

I hate it when someone asks me this question. *The* cause of autism hasn't been determined or declared yet. But now that you know how varied autism can be, you have a basis to understand the difficulty. There are likely many causes of autism. Because autism is simply a description of certain symptoms that qualify for a diagnosis, each of these symptoms could, perhaps, have different causation. Perhaps the autism that affects children who can speak and have no digestive tract problems has a different cause than the autism that affects non-verbal children, or children who are greatly helped with diet changes.

Many parents and professionals have long held the belief that children with autism are born with a predisposition to the disorder. It is then triggered by something in the environment, such as a toxic chemical exposure. In May 2000, a syndicated Los Angeles Times article reported such a medical finding—that research indicates a predisposition to autism is present at birth. "A team from the California Birth Defects Monitoring program examined stored blood samples from 249 infants collected during the 1980s. The researchers found unusually high levels of four proteins associated with brain development in nearly all the samples from children who later were diagnosed with autism or retardation, but in none from infants who developed normally."[9] This is one of the most exciting pieces of autism research I have ever read. The article went on to say that this finding does not rule out other more immediate causal factors, such as vaccinations. However, it may soon be possible to screen newborns for these proteins and counsel parents of infants with the predisposition. If the medical community begins to take autism prevention seriously, these parents will be cautioned to avoid possible symptom triggers, such as those I mention in the rest of this chapter.

There are many parents whose children's autism was clearly triggered by the MMR vaccine. Yet Lauren already had symptoms of autism before receiving this vaccine. Lauren did have a severe reaction to her DTP shot. She slept for two days. She hardly woke for the feedings I forced her to take every three hours. It is only within the last few years that there has been much discussion about the DTP as a cause of autism. It's actually not the vaccine itself, but the preservative that has been used with the vaccine (and which is part of the shot put into the child's body) that is suspect. The amount of mercury in the preservative is of toxic levels even to adults. Chelation therapy (which removes heavy metals like mercury from the body) has helped many people with autism. I am looking forward to reading more research and wonder if this may one day help Lauren.[10]

Lauren undeniably has yeast problems, and has improved drastically by our addressing these problems. Even when Lauren was first diagnosed, every professional knew that, for some reason, autism tended to parallel high incidence of ear infections, and subsequently, frequent antibiotic use. (Antibiotics attack all bacteria in the body, even the ones needed to stay healthy, which creates the yeast imbalance in the child's system.) Yet, there are certainly children out there who have had many ear infections, but no autism.

I know one thing for sure. Lauren was once a perfectly healthy baby with terrific social skills and she slowly changed. I avoid eighteen months worth of photos in my albums. It's too painful to see so obviously what we didn't see as it was unnoticeably unfolding. I wonder every now and then if I at some point made a decision that is responsible for Lauren's autism. I believe I did, but if so, I did it without hesitation. I had studied child development in college and as a new mother. I explicitly followed every piece of advice given to me by my children's medical doctors. I trusted that, at every moment, I was doing what was best for my children's physical, mental and emotional health. Whenever someone tells me, "I don't know anything about autism," I reply, "I didn't either, until I had to. There's absolutely no reason anyone would unless they were somehow affected by it."

Well, now I am affected by it day-in and day-out, minute to minute. I now think about it and read about it more frequently than I think about or read about anything else. So, of course, I now have some suspicions and some strongly held beliefs about what is responsible for autism. But I also know there is at least one autism "expert" out there who could come up with statistics that would make my suspicions and beliefs sound ridiculous. (It's amazing what people can do with statistics. Craig and I love hearing reports of new research results, then counting the ways one set of numbers are "interpreted" by various groups. Omitting corroborating evidence in order to downplay results or not discussing the criteria of control groups, for example, are just two ways to make definitive statistics say exactly what you want.)

I'm going to completely avoid the criticism of my "betters" with many letters after their names and remind you that this is a mother's story. I may not have the authority to suggest what causes autism, but I have the authority to make the best choices I know how to make for my children. I can't remake some pivotal decisions of Lauren's past, but I will share with you anyway what I would do differently if I had another opportunity. I have no plans to have another child to prove my sincerity, so you'll have to decide for yourself if this information has any bearing on your life.

If I were to have another baby, I would do nothing differently than I did last time during my pregnancy with Lauren. OK, maybe I would avoid spraying Pledge on that shelf—the one where most of the Pledge missed the shelf and settled on the linoleum floor beneath the chair I was standing on. When I stepped down, my feet slipped out from underneath me and my behind hit the floor hard. I was five months pregnant at the time, but the doctor said that the baby was well padded and if there wasn't bleeding, I shouldn't worry. There wasn't bleeding, but I would like to have avoided that fall anyway!

If I were to do it all again, I would again breastfeed my babies as long as they would let me (or until I couldn't stand it any more, whichever came first).

I would not immunize my babies at all, with any vaccination, until they had an impressive vocabulary and had met every developmental milestone that has a space for a date next to it in the baby book. When I did finally choose to vaccinate for some disease that my pediatrician convinced me was of a significant danger (the lectures can't be helped—they come with most medical degrees) I would require to know all the ingredients of the vaccine and anything else included in the syringe that goes into the child, such as preservatives. I would not agree to any vaccine with any toxic substance, such as mercury, in its recipe. I would allow only one vaccine to be given at a time—no combinations. (Yes, that is possible. It's just not standard or most cost effective.) If there are going to be side effects, I like to know what to blame. I'm amazed by moms who worry about combining children's cough medicine, cold medicine and pain killer, but they allow a combination drug with much more potential danger attached to it to be administered to their children with no questions asked.

I would make sure that my child is as healthy as possible when any vaccine is administered. Yes, that means that I might have to schedule an extra appointment rather than let the doctor vaccinate during a checkup where an ear infection or red throat is discovered. I'm more than willing to be inconvenienced. When I talk to my friends who are trying to decide when to vaccinate, they always say, "But the doctor and the nurses treat me like I'm ignorant and paranoid when I say I'd like to wait. I never know what to say." I tell them, "Be very sweet and soft spoken and say, 'I'd be happy to vaccinate Junior today, but I'll need a signed guarantee from you that if he is ever diagnosed with autism, you'll pay all his medical, therapy and education fees.' Most doctors will say, 'No,' and you can just agree, saying, 'OK, then, we'll do it on my schedule.' If your child's doctor has a bold or impulsive personality and no respect for the individual rights of parents to deem what's right for their children, then you might want to have such a contract typed up and ready to hand him or her."

If I were to do it all again, I would never give my child antibiotics except under these circumstances:

1. The child has reached all milestones listed in his/her baby book[11] and/or

2. The child has seen a chiropractor specializing in children and has had her spine adjusted on a regular basis, if needed.[12]

3. I have tried all natural remedies for the infection and nothing has worked.

If I did decide to give my child antibiotics, I would also give high doses of a healthy flora supplement while he or she was taking it and for a while afterward. If one round of antibiotics didn't clear up the infection, I would try every other means possible to rid the infection. I would know that the correlation of a child losing hearing to a popped eardrum is much lower than the correlation of autism symptoms to repeated antibiotic use. I would reassure myself with this knowledge, and with the knowledge that having a hearing impairment would seem like vacation in Aruba compared to having autism like Lauren's, to both the child and the parents.[13]

I would do my best to serve meat and animal byproducts that are antibiotic and hormone-free. If I'm going to actively avoid inserting antibiotics into my child, I'm not going to passively let him or her get a regular dosage.

I would keep my child away from dairy products as much as possible (meaning that we would definitely still have an occasional Dairy Queen cone or dish of Ben & Jerry's). As soon as my child experienced repeated sinus infections or ear infections, I would even eliminate the occasional ice cream treat.

I would be aware of all molds and mildews in my child's environment, then get rid of their sources as soon as possible. I would avoid use of all chemicals in my home which are unnecessary, such as pesticides and cleaning solutions. I would realize that most household chemicals are unnecessary and replaceable by even more effective natural substances.

I would serve my family as few artificial ingredients as possible in their food. If my child began exhibiting bizarre or troubling behavior, I would keep a log of everything he or she has eaten. If I realized any correlation between behavior and food, I would try an elimination diet.

You probably realize by now that some of these things I am doing under the *better late than never* rule. Lauren has been drastically helped by changes in diet. We've also eliminated most chemicals in our home. Lauren had an obvious and immediate reaction to some, so it made sense to eliminate as many as we could. Considering that she puts many items she finds in her mouth, this has frequently provided us a sense of relief.

Of course, there are some days when we fall off the path of best intentions. When money is tight, we sometimes take short cuts; or when Lauren's begging for something that's not healthy for her, we might give in and begin to question whether there's really any harm done by it anyway. But a change in Lauren's behavior or health consistently puts us right back on track.

So, here it is—a mother's dissertation. I don't know for sure what causes autism. I don't know why some people are susceptible, while others exposed to near duplicate conditions are not. But I know that if I'm traveling on roads reputed to have poisonous snakes cross them, I'm going to plot the most safe and direct route possible, keep my eyes to the road and have a first aid kit handy. This is the best map and first aid kit I know to give you, though I hope we can pack a better one very soon.

What's Her Prognosis?

P eople didn't ask me this question when Lauren was younger. She was quiet and small. Everyone was reassuring, even those with no knowledge of autism or Lauren would reassure me that I was a terrific mother and that Lauren would be fine. As she grew larger, noisier and some of her behaviors became more obvious, people more often asked, "How's she doing?" and "What's her prognosis?"

I remember the day I realized that it's pretty accepted form not to assume anything about our children's future, as our plans and assumptions can serve to limit them. I also realized that no one asks me what I think Bryn's future will be like. They certainly never ask me about her prognosis. But if they did, my answer would be the same short answer I now give when they ask about Lauren. I say, "If all goes as expected, she's definitely going to grow up to be a woman."

School

Our family's experience with school has been diverse and ever-changing. When Lauren was first diagnosed, I went to a parent support group one evening. While there, I informed other attendees that my husband and I had just checked out a preschool program for children with autism at a local prestigious university. Everyone there knew of this program and some said, "Oh, if they'll take you, go, go, go!" A few moms remained quiet at the time. I signed Lauren up the next day and she began attending the following Monday. She attended for eight days.

On Day One, Lauren walked into the classroom, found a corner away from the other children and tucked herself quietly into a fetal position on the floor. Lauren was usually happy and explorative, so this amazed me. This was the first impression had by the teachers, so they did not know that my daughter characteristically acted (at twenty-two months old) more like a normal, albeit quiet, little toddler.

I was new to the world of autism, so my learning had just begun. I met with another therapist, Marian, the first week Lauren was in that program and told her about Lauren's experience in the classroom. She suggested that we give the program thirteen days. If we didn't see any improvement in the situation in thirteen days, then we should pull her out. She said any situation that is good for Lauren should look good after giving it about thirteen days. (I've used the thirteen-day rule quite a bit since then. I think Marian just pulled the number thirteen out of thin air. I think twelve days or two weeks would be as good a marker, but thirteen has been the number I've remembered and used ever since then.) I later found out that this therapist did not approve of many of the theories this preschool program put into practice. However, she was respectful enough of other professionals and of me not to denigrate the institution, but to let me see for myself and make my own judgements independently. She gave me articles written by Temple Grandin, an adult with autism, and suggested some other autobiographical works by people with autism. (The preschool program had not provided or recommended any educational material.) I also found out later that a few moms at the support group meeting I attended never would have put their children in the program for reasons similar to Marian's, but I was just learning.

On Day Two of Lauren's preschool program, Lauren wandered over to one of the teachers and reached up to him with her arms. I was observing through a two-way mirror and I saw my precious child reach to an adult for the first time! But the teacher was busy with another child, so he turned Lauren around and pushed her in another direction. My child reached a milestone at twenty-two months that most babies do in their first six months and she didn't receive the natural response (someone picking her up) that would encourage her to continue to reach out to others in this way. From behind the glass, my heart ached that she wasn't home right then, where Mommy would have realized the significance of this event and celebrated by picking her up, praising her and dancing around the room with her. I wrote the head teacher a long note about this occurrence. I explained that Lauren had never reached for anyone before and how she must be picked up when it happens, to reinforce the behavior. I watched on another day from the window for just a few minutes when I arrived to pick up Lauren. The children had just come inside from playing. One teacher was taking turns with each child, removing his or her shoes and putting on his or her slippers. After getting Lauren's slippers on her feet, the teacher set her in motion toward the classroom. But Lauren turned around, walked over to him and reached her arms up to him to have him pick her up. (It was her usual nap time, so I knew she wanted comfort in her sleepiness.) The man turned her back around and pushed her toward the classroom again as he had to attend to the shoes and slippers of the next of a dozen children. My baby walked away, having been shown once again that when she (at twenty-two months old) is tired or sad and wants the comfort of an adult's arms, reaching for that adult to express the need is not the way to get it met!

I was in a state of confusion. I felt that every plan I ever had for mothering my children had been desecrated. My baby was in the car with my husband at 6:30 A.M., despite the fact that she didn't naturally wake up until about 8:00 A.M. I was trying to feed her when she wasn't yet hungry so she could get out the door to conquer traffic on the twenty-five mile trek to her school. My three-year-old ate peanut butter and jelly in the car every day as we drove the same twenty-five miles to pick up her sister. It was an hour-and-a-half round trip. Our lives were centered around "school" when I had never had plans to send my children to school. We already had been planning to homeschool at this time, so we certainly had not planned on preschool. But I was new to the world of autism. Having no expertise to fall back on, I deferred to "the experts"—some people who at least had experience with autism.

On the first day of Lauren's attendance in this program, I knew nothing about the many and varied sensory challenges faced by people with autism. One day, I was so unhappy about the turn our family's life had taken, and so angry that I was doing what was completely against my mothering instinct, that I was being unbearable to my family. Craig finally ushered me to the door at lunchtime and said, "You're going out to eat by yourself. Take as much time as you need." (Isn't that a terrific way to handle a mother who's being beastly? I'll never forget that day and I fall in love with my husband again every time I think of it.) I took the literature Marian had given me and finally sat down, in a public restaurant, to take time to read it. (Any mom can appreciate that having information is good, but having the time to read it is the only way it's useful!)

I read about Temple Grandin and many of her sensory experiences as a child. Temple described the type of classroom that was useful to her learning and the kind that was chaotic and forced her to "shut down." I realized that Lauren was shutting down in the classroom because of the overwhelming environment. It was a very large room with skylights, tables, chairs, centers for various activities, large windows and an average of sixteen people in there at any one time. By the second week, Lauren would become very upset when her Dad arrived at the classroom door. She would try to drag him away from it. After reading this material, I didn't blame my daughter a bit for not wanting to set foot across that threshold. Over the years, Lauren's particular sensory needs and challenges have become obvious to us and we would never expect her to enter such a situation without a lot of preparation and support. That there was a time when her dad and I weren't aware of her needs seems like a very distant memory now.

During her second week of school, Lauren still remained in her own little world, except when on the playground (and when at home and most places outside the classroom, of course). She boggled her teachers, who evidently had not encountered children with as challenging sensory needs as Lauren's. The teachers were trained in behavioral management, but their behavioral techniques couldn't work on a child who rarely opened her eyes or moved from one spot because the environment was too intimidating. A teacher came to our house for the first home visit and was amazed at Lauren's sociability in her home. She complimented many of the "strategies" I had implemented (though at the time they were just parenting choices), then told me that the teachers and administrators at the school had brainstormed about Lauren at their last staff meeting. They had all noticed that Lauren was very comfortable, loving and most outgoing while in my arms (surprise, surprise) and they wanted to use this "interest" of hers. The teacher asked me if there was anything that Lauren would associate with Mommy, any perfume that they could spray on a blanket, for example. I didn't wear perfume, but I asked why. The staff had decided that they would give some "Mommy object" to Lauren whenever she made a positive overture, such as if she moved toward where other children were play-ing. "Then what would happen?" I asked.

"We would take the Mommy object away after a short time. Then when she did something positive again, we would give it to her again." This teaching method seemed to make so much sense to this young teacher that I didn't want to burst her bubble with my many doubts, so I remained quiet. I couldn't help thinking some reasonable thoughts like, "Wouldn't taking the wonderful, unconditionally loving relation-ship in Lauren's life and making it conditional be more likely to destroy that relationship than to make her do your will?"

On Lauren's last day at the preschool, we met with the program director and voiced our concerns about Lauren's sensory needs not being addressed. I told the woman some facts and theories that I had read and how I found them applicable to Lauren. The director told us that she did not share the same theories as the people whose books and articles I had been reading. I found it amusing that she doubted the autobiographical experiences of people with autism, when she doesn't have autism. In the end, we respectfully agreed to disagree, and Craig and I told her that these were the reasons we were removing Lauren from the program. The ride home with our whole family in the car was one of the most joyful rides we've ever taken. I knew by this time that I would never again deny my mother's instinct or ignore my family's basic priorities when choosing what is best for Lauren.

When I speak with parents who are looking at various educational settings for their children with autism, I give them one piece of advice: Whatever you imagined your life with this child to look like before he or she was diagnosed, try to stay as close to that as possible. I had vol-unteered in a daycare center when I was in college and, compared to my experience of toddler daycare, the university preschool program was a very good daycare. Children without autism were also in the classrooms as peer models, so the program would have taken Bryn, too. If I had intended to work and have my children in daycare, this would have met my vision for my family very nicely.

I had not intended to work outside the home while my children were young. Many women would be indignant at the suggestion that their career end because they had a child. Yet I was supposed to accept that my intended career, being a full-time mom, had to end because my child had autism. For a mom with an ideal of working outside the home and having children, this program could keep that dream alive, despite autism. For me, it was an institution keeping me from all my ideals, from my career, from my children.

The reason Lauren was in the preschool for eight days instead of two whole weeks is because she was out sick with conjunctivitis for a day or two. I was very upset when she came down with it as it's very contagious and the remedy is difficult. When the whole family came down with it, putting drops in Bryn's and Lauren's eyes was like wrestling a rhino to take its horn. I took Lauren back to class when she was no longer contagious. You can imagine how angry I was upon seeing another little girl with obvious masses of gook draining out of both eyes. This should be another consideration when deciding whether to put your child in a daycare-like setting. Even if you're a conscientious parent who will keep your child away when sick, not all parents are as conscientious, and your family pays the price. I've discovered over the years how very susceptible Lauren is to illness, so I'm especially grateful for the limited-germ benefit of homeschooling.

That's one of the first things I looked for in Lauren's later schooling experiences. Teachers and administrators need to respect Lauren's unique health needs. Sleep is one of her greatest needs. Over the years when Lauren was falling asleep at 3:00 A.M. or waking up at 5:00 A.M. (and some nights doing both) her school program had to be flexible. After her worst nights, her teachers and therapists needed to give her a place to rest, give her an easy day and understand that this was a symptom of her autism, rather than blaming mom.

Until we solved many of Lauren's allergy problems, Lauren often had a cold and was usually congested. One of her first speech therapists became quite disgusted by the situation. We had to cancel frequently because we considered Lauren contagious. I knew this didn't please the therapist, so I was happy one day when we kept her appointment because Lauren just had the sniffles, no full-blown cold. At the end of Lauren's session, the therapist came out and said with a frown on her face, "You shouldn't bring her when she has the sniffles. I could get sick. Then I wouldn't be able to see the rest of my clients!" All I could think was, "You're the adult. You know not to put the toys in your mouth. Buy some Lysol and use it!" But instead of saying anything, we soon found another therapist who knew not to put the toys in her mouth and whose criteria for contagious were closer to ours. This therapist is still with us, so she's been a first-hand witness to amazing improvements in Lauren's health as we've tried new approaches.

The distance a family has to travel to a school program is also important. While I felt it was wrong that our family's days seemed solely dedicated to getting Lauren to and from school, it was leading another family to serious problems. One mom I met at the preschool was driving one and a half hours each way. Her son had autism and was in the program. Her daughter was older than Bryn and was becoming depressed. The little girl typically stayed with friends while her mother did the driving. The mom felt like she never saw her daughter, because, of course, her son's needs didn't end when they arrived home. The woman told me her husband and she were having serious problems. She felt the crux of their problems was her own unhappiness about her day-to-day existence. This woman took her son out of the program soon after we removed Lauren, for many of the same reasons. I saw her at a few conferences later and her family was much happier. Life was still difficult, but the family was stronger and happier because mom was home more and better able to meet everyone's needs, including her own.

Another thing I've learned over the years about choosing schooling for Lauren is that if it's right for her, it will also be affordable. This may sound backward, like it should read: If it's affordable, it's right for her. That's not what I mean. Public school may be affordable for everyone, but that doesn't mean that it's right for everyone. However, if a program or treatment will cost money that the family doesn't have (and in this credit-card-happy society, I think everyone knows how you can pay with money you don't have) then it's not right for the child right now. One of the regrets I have about the decisions we've made over the years is that we accrued debt to try things that ended up not helping Lauren. I would never judge a person who did the same thing, as I probably wouldn't regret the expenditure if Lauren had been helped! Also, many people say there is a window of opportunity when children with autism are young. Craig and I like to think that we tried everything we possibly could for Lauren and didn't miss any window of opportunity. However, I think that if we had been a little more patient and waited on what God wanted for our family, we would have been better directed and spent our money in a wiser fashion. I like to think that is exactly what we do now, not that we've just given up hope or are getting cheap in our old age!

People often ask me what has helped Lauren the most. The first and biggest breakthrough in communication came for Lauren after I read the book, *Sonrise.* I was considering trying the Options Institute methods of therapy. The premise of this therapy is to constantly follow the child's lead, copying her behavior. While others are trying to break into her world, the child will develop interest in these persistent human beings and break out into their world. Lauren was in her own little world much of the day at this time. The antics of her sister didn't even interest her at this age—just after her second birthday—the way they had when she was a baby. Her days were spent in activity such as: studying her own hands, studying the fur on her stuffed animals, running her hands through plastic bicycle streamers, scooting backwards in circles on the floor and watching Disney videos.

Lauren loved to go outside into the backyard, where we had a swing set and a toddler jungle gym. But Lauren ignored the swings and toys. Left to her own devices, she ran circles around the entire yard. Sometimes she would run her hand along the fence, the house or a tree as she zoomed past, but she rarely stopped to rest. One day, I watched Lauren as she ran in her circle, then I suddenly stood up and followed. I ran closely behind her and tried to keep up with her, touching the fence, house and trees where she had touched them. Lauren laughed! She kept looking back slightly as she ran and seemed excited that I was there. Finally, (probably after only two or three laps, I'm in such great shape) I sat back down on the two-person swing where I had started out. Lauren finished one more circle, then came over to me at the swing. She looked me in the eye with a huge smile across her face, took me by the arm and dragged me to my feet. When I started running again, she laughed again. I felt I knew what that huge smile meant: "You get it, don't you?! You finally understand!" I think I only made it around one full circle this time, when I sat down. Lauren immediately came over to me and pulled on my arm again. When I told her Mommy was tired and didn't budge, she walked behind me and pushed on my back to get me going in the right direction! I couldn't resist such well communicated instruction, so I dragged myself around another lap and sat again. Despite how thrilled I was with the interaction, I didn't budge the next time. Bryn was sitting next to me at the moment. After a minute or two of attempts at persuading me, Lauren turned to Bryn, dragged her to her feet, pushed her and they were off! I felt like crying, but the exhaustion from running kept me just watching the two of them, filled with joy at what I had witnessed. Lauren had asked her sister to come play with her for the first time.

The second greatest "breakthrough" with Lauren has had to do with music. I don't remember any specific event which made me realize music was so powerful. There was simply and naturally a gradual building of its uses in Lauren's therapy and in our lives. I do remember that Lauren's first phrase was "Rudolph the Red Nosed Reindeer" said in a sing-songy fashion immediately after Burl Ives sang the song in Lauren's *Rudolph* video. I also recall one of Lauren's and my lengthiest verbal interactions. I began to sing the Alphabet song to her, leaving off half of each phrase. Of course she'd heard the song hundreds of times, so when I sang "ABCD" and she quietly responded "EFG", I shouldn't have been so surprised. I kept going, right through to Lauren's "next time won't you sing with me" (which sounded more like neh tah woh yuh suh wuh weh" but Mommy knew exactly what she meant!) I sing some beautiful songs with my church band, but this was undoubtedly the most moving singing experience I've ever had.

I discuss the power of music in the chapter called Empowerment. I've often felt instant comfort with a new teacher or therapist when they've asked, "What about music? Does Lauren respond to music?" If they mention it early on in the relationship, they have probably experienced breakthrough moments with children using music. The theory behind music as I see it is (much like the Options Institute theory): "When you can't get in, drag her out (or intrigue her) with music." I look for this use of music in any good classroom/therapy situation. If a therapist doesn't understand how music will help Lauren, then she probably doesn't understand Lauren.

Families can go to the Options Institute to learn their practices. They offer programs in a retreat style setting in the Northeast. Attendance costs a few thousand dollars, however, so Craig and I never attended. (This was one time we chose not to overextend ourselves financially.) We did read paperwork from the Options Institute and met with other families who had attended. We then set up a version of the program in our home. We put all of Lauren's toys up high on shelves so she would have to communicate in order to ask for them. We found volunteers through a church bulletin advertisement and taught them the techniques we had learned. They began coming by one at a time for an hour at a time to help us keep Lauren busy as many hours of the day as possible. We were trying to pull her into our world and keep her in our world.

The volunteers who lasted more than a month (I think many thought it would be more like babysitting and a lot less work) became dear family friends. They filled out paperwork so we could keep track of progress. I remember the first time one of the women heard Lauren say the word "swing" clearly. You would have thought the sky had just rained dimes, she was so excited. I was happy, too, but I think as much from my new friend's joy at being part of the moment as from Lauren's accomplishment.

Having volunteers in our home was difficult, particularly as most of the volunteers were people with full-time jobs, so they had to come after work or on weekends. Lauren was often tired by the time people came by, or we wanted to just do family activities when Dad had his weekends off from work. (I'm sure the Options Institute stresses what kind of people and hours to schedule in order to avoid this situation.) We needed to reduce the number of hours, and therefore, the number of people who came by. About one year after starting the program, we only had two people still coming by and our primary therapy hours for Lauren were not volunteer hours.

Even before we had volunteers come into our home, we had been attending therapy with Marian. Marian's methodology was much like the university preschool Lauren had attended, but she addressed the sensory needs of the individual child. Her classrooms were much smaller. Lauren started out seeing her one-to-one or with Bryn present as a peer model. Marian believed theory was secondary to what worked. She had many years of experience with people with autism and had many approaches up her sleeve. She was a loving therapist, then a terrific consultant as we reduced the number of hours Lauren attended. (Marian's program was thirty miles away on a route with horrific traffic, so we stayed closer to home as we began meeting Lauren's needs closer to home.)

Lauren has seen three different speech therapists over the years and four different occupational therapists. Her current speech therapist has been with us since Lauren was five and has many of the same qualities as Marian. She loves my child; she's not stuck on a theory, but is open-minded to what works specifically for Lauren; and she's a great consultant. (Good teachers and therapists also tend to be good consultants, as they want to have any progress cross over into the child's entire life in any setting. They also care about the family's health and happiness.)

Lauren attended our local public school for five months during what would be her second grade year. I sought a new school setting for her because we had been through a horrible summer and I had lost all creativity and energy. (It was the first summer that we could no longer go to the pool because Lauren can't tolerate the chemicals,[14] and summers are extremely hot where we live.) Craig and I observed a number of classrooms in some potential settings, but we chose a special ed classroom in the local school she would attend if she were in a regular second grade class. The class was made up mostly of children more physically impaired than Lauren, and one boy with autism, who reminded us a lot of Lauren. We chose it because of the teacher and the environment. Music played often. It was a peaceful classroom where the activities were more along the line of preschool activities. (In the more advanced special ed classes, we pictured Lauren stimming[15] often while other children recited their ABC's and Math facts.) The best thing about the class, however, was Lauren's teacher. She knew a great deal about autism, she treated Craig and me like we were the experts on our child, and she genuinely loved and enjoyed the children she taught. (Most of these qualities were not evident in any of the other teachers we observed.)

Lauren left the public school classroom when the teachers kept sending her home early because of her behavior. I wasn't laughing at the time, but I think back and laugh at the situation: Many people have encouraged me over the years to put Lauren in school as though that's where she'll get expert care and help. In school, Lauren had a personal teacher's aide, and two other teachers were in the classroom, but when they couldn't handle her behavior, they sent her home. I guess they thought I had magic powers or something.

At the same time that Lauren's classroom seemed no longer suitable for her, we found out her beloved teacher (who was the reason we chose that classroom) was leaving to move to another state. Had we decided to keep Lauren in school, the school system agreed with us that her current classroom was no longer right for her. Craig and I observed the only other classroom that might be "right" for Lauren. The classroom was a sensory nightmare. There were so many cubicles for various activities, I felt like a rat in a maze, even being tall enough to see that daylight did exist somewhere beyond the final half wall. We also think Hitler would have loved what they called the "time-out" room—I think it used to be an elevator shaft. When we turned on the light, a very loud fan came on and the noise of it bounced off the cinderblock walls, echoing in a fashion that instantly hurt even my not-so-sensitive ears. We suspected Lauren would be spending a great deal of time in time-out, so we decided to keep her home where her time-out room is carpeted and has a soft bed in it. We could have fought the school system to create a more appropriate placement for Lauren, but there was negativity from the start of discussions and I knew from experience that when we're fighting the outside world, the world inside our home is tense and unhappy. I didn't know how long such a fight would take, but the promise of its end wasn't great enough to risk the peace and sanctity of our home and family. I began, once again, to create a homeschool that meets Lauren's needs.

There are many things I've learned from Lauren's various educational experiences that have reinforced my belief that she's usually best off being taught at home. One of these things is that it takes a long time to understand the needs of any one child, as well as to develop a trusting relationship with that child so she's willing and able to work with you. Two teachers and three therapists who have worked with Lauren possessed this understanding and developed such a relationship. Whenever a teacher or therapist changes, the relationship is all new and must start from scratch. New teachers walking into Lauren's life need to minimally get a grip on some basic facts, such as that Lauren is an "eloper" (an escape artist). She must constantly have firm boundaries and supervision or there is a real danger of our losing her. She tends not to come when called and has little appreciation for the danger of things like oncoming cars, so this danger must be taken seriously.

During one summer program Lauren attended, I helped out by teaching another classroom of older children. One day, from my classroom I heard Lauren's teacher and an older student walking quickly down hallways in opposite directions and calling out, "Lauren! Lauren!" I knew instantly that they had lost my daughter. I thought about the proximity of the street and the train tracks and I ran to join in the search. I found Lauren in a hallway, almost to an outer door. I had put Lauren into this classroom having reservations about this new teacher's capability to understand and work with my daughter. Maybe those reservations were premature, but it seems she would have to understand and provide for her basic safety before she could progress to an understanding of the way Lauren's mind operates.

At home, Lauren's teachers (Mom, Dad and Bryn) are never starting from scratch. We are always working with her from the context of a deep, multi-faceted relationship. Sometimes this may be a bad thing, such as when Lauren knows which buttons to push to get Mom mad so she'll stop an activity. But once her motivations and ploys are discovered, there are ways around them. We're building endlessly upon knowledge and successes previously gained. At home, we have a flexible budget (with only Dad needing to approve any expenditure) and a flexible environment. We've been known to add cubicle walls, move major appliances and cut holes in doors to make things work. We'll do anything to meet Lauren's needs because it's *our* lives at stake. Our family can't be happy when one of our own is unhappy or failing at what she strives to do or be. Lauren's educational successes and failures are our family's successes and failures. That's a daunting prospect (imagine if every school teacher had that burden for every student) but it's true. That's why our school will do whatever is possible to help our students be successful.

Another positive aspect of homeschooling Lauren has been that I know what goes on in her day. If anything negative happens during the school day, a non-verbal child can't come home and tell Mom and Dad about it. It's a fact of life that non-verbal people are victims of various forms of abuse because they're the perfect victims—they can't identify their suspect, or even the crime. There were many days when Lauren got into the car after school and was so upset that I couldn't settle her down for hours. I don't believe that anyone has ever intentionally physically hurt my child, but I've left a mark on her body from my firm grip a number of times when I was holding her back from hurting others or from running off. It's one thing when Mom does it, but if a stranger handles her roughly, she would want Mom to know and would have some anger or sadness about it. I'm sure no one has ever intended to verbally abuse her, either. But I have walked into the classroom unannounced and heard teachers speaking about Lauren, in her presence, in a harsh and angry way. Perhaps Lauren doesn't seem to understand what they're saying, but her behavior after such an incident suggests that she is very hurt and has no means to express her hurt. Just avoiding such ills is another huge benefit to keeping Lauren's education in the hands of a small group whose own hearts hurt when Lauren is hurting.

I'm obviously very supportive of homeschooling, but as I said early in this chapter, you should strive to raise your family after the autism diagnosis as closely as possible to the ideal you held before the diagnosis. If you always planned on having your children in public school or in a private religious school, I hope you'll first see if that will still work. Not all children with an autism diagnosis have as many challenges as Lauren, and I know of some private schools that strive to meet the needs of special needs students as those needs arise. I hope when looking at the value of a program for your child, you'll take what you know works for your child and compare it to what the program offers. There's a good chance that if you think the program is missing something in the beginning, that missing thing will become a big problem as time goes on. It might be a good idea to address it from the start.

After years of working with Lauren, I have my own list of qualities I look for in a program. I've alluded to some of these already, such as respect for parents and their ideas. I look for a daily form of communication between parent and teacher. A notebook that is sent back and forth, so parents and teacher can write about the child's accomplishments or difficulties, is one form I've found useful when the teacher reads it first thing and writes in it daily. I look for respect for the child's health needs. Do teachers stress getting the child there on time over letting the child get extra sleep in the morning if she was up all night? Do they respect the parents' choices regarding the child's health, such as immunization choices and any chemical or other sensitivities they want avoided? Do they guarantee the child's special diet requirements will be followed?

I look for affordability and proximity, as I mentioned. If you have to move to have your child attend the program you believe is best for him or her, great. Just take your whole family and be a whole family in your new location. Don't let autism break up your family. It's not what God wants and it's not what you want. And even more than being in the best educational setting in the world, every child wants his or her family all together in one home.

In my observations of a classroom or therapy setting, I look for a positive environment. Read the chapter called "Positive Environment" and the ones following it to fully understand the qualities of a positive environment: Respect (for the student), Empathy, Empowerment and Laughter. Laughter has been a big part of my relationship with Lauren's best teachers and therapists. If I can't laugh with someone who works with Lauren about the wild world of autism and the crazy ways it affects every activity, then I probably am not going to keep him or her around long. People who understand have senses of humor. That's all there is to it.

I look for as little down time, or stim time, as possible. This might mean there's a high ratio of teacher to student, or that the child spends a lot of time with therapists who work one-to-one. A high ratio of teacher to student doesn't mean much if the teachers don't have a firm understanding of your child and his personal needs. Know who will actually be with your child most of the day. I found that Lauren's beloved public school teacher was more often out for IEP[16] meetings and other administrative duties than in the classroom. (I wish I could have hired her to work one-to-one with Lauren in my home, as her expertise and enthusiasm weren't of much use while she was sitting in administrative meetings.)

I also look for some specific educational methods I know work best with Lauren. It may take some observation of the child's classroom time to ascertain what methods are actually and consistently being used. *Backwards chaining*[17] is one method that has worked with Lauren very well. In the more common practice of *chaining*, a skill is taught in its natural sequence. For example, to teach a child to set the table, you would first have her put out all the place mats on the empty table, then have her bring out the plates, etc. To teach a child to set the table using backwards chaining, you would go through all the steps while she watches, then have her do the last step, such as bring out the platter of food, if that's the last step at your house. (We fill our plates in the kitchen and Lauren will gladly bring out a plate of food, as then she can eat! Using natural motivation is quite helpful!) Backwards chaining is at work when you hear a child say the last word of every phrase in a song before she can sing the whole song. Backwards chaining is helpful to many people with autism who have a hard time processing verbal instruction because they have many cues to help them understand the situation while they're in the early stages of learning. The visual cue of an almost fully set table is more easily understood than someone pointing to an empty table while requesting that it be set. The purpose and sequence is much easier to grasp when the person has walked through the process a number of times before.

To picture the idea of backwards chaining, I think of myself putting together a bunch of cars to a Brio train, starting with the engine and adding one at a time until I get to the caboose. By the time I'm ready for the caboose, I can hand it to Lauren and say, "Put it on" and she will know exactly how to do that. The next time I build it, I'll hand her the second to last car and then the caboose. Soon, she'll have witnessed the process enough to be able to build the whole train when I hand her the engine. People often naturally use this process when teaching a child to stack blocks, asking the child to put the last block on after he has seen that the goal is to put the blocks in a row on top of each other. This simple process can be used in more complicated tasks like toilet training, writing a name or numbers in sequence, or learning a job skill.

Another educational method related to backwards chaining is what I call "Input, Input, Input!" People like my Lauren often don't perform well when called upon to prove their knowledge or understanding. Lauren doesn't perform tasks consistently, so it's hard to gauge her true understanding of a verbal request or her mastery of a skill. The best therapists and teachers, however, maintain their trust in her capability despite her moment-to-moment performance and keep giving her more and more "input." They give her books to look at and talk about with new topics that they think will intrigue her. They try new themes and repeat old themes that were favorites so that Lauren constantly has information entering her brain, hopefully gaining more and more significance. I equate this with backwards chaining because both are methods based on the foundational belief that the more meaningful information that the child is exposed to, the more likely she'll be able to put that information to use when she is better able to communicate or to understand context. More simply put: If we never show her anything, why should she talk? She doesn't have anything to talk about!

If you can't imagine any other type of educational method, picture this: A teacher says, "We worked on the letter A today, but she still won't say or point to any words with the letter A in them. So, we'll be working on that again tomorrow. Oh, and the color of the week is still red for the eighth week in a row because she still hasn't said or pointed to the word 'red'." I call this the "Bore them to death till they do die" method of teaching. I have seen glimpses of this in classrooms I have observed. Sometimes, otherwise good teachers may fall into this rut when they become discouraged and just want some encouragement from the student that *something, anything* is getting through. Sometimes, just pointing out evidence of the student's slow but steady progress is enough to get the teacher past the discouragement and on to better ways of teaching. (The teacher in my example may be too far gone, however!)

Once a child is in an educational program, one good way to judge its value and effectiveness is just by looking at the child's behavior at home. Is she exhausted and moody while at home? Is she joyful, or at least no less joyful than before she began the program? Of course, an initial transition period is to be expected. Consider using the thirteen-day rule if you suspect that the program is having a negative effect on the child's behavior. If the child's teacher reports that she is content and successful at school, ask for the teacher's help in carrying school routines over into the home environment. For example, if there is a period of quiet time with music playing after lunch each day, try to recreate that at home on the weekends and holidays. If the child seems to benefit from lots of physical activity early in the day, try to provide opportunity for similar activity on the mornings of her days off from school. If a child is making color choices by choosing what color plate she wants at lunchtime, buy some colored plates for home. A good teacher will be cooperative and happy that you value your child's experience at school and want to recreate it at home.

Of course, if you find yourself or your child in a negative school situation that seems beyond repair, remember my rule for negative people: *Ditch 'em!* You don't have time for them. Find other people who are loving and helpful. They're out there if you look. I've met quite a few of them.

Alternative[18] Medicine, Diet and Sleep

When Lauren was first diagnosed, I think I believed that her difficulties would just be something I would have to teach to, as I would a child with dyslexia or some other learning disorder. Even the pediatric neurologist who diagnosed Lauren told us that the best thing we could do to help her was to find a strong educational program for her. She was so docile and quiet back then, I couldn't have imagined how very wrong the doctor could be, or how very difficult that "prescription" would be to fill. The doctor was excited when, on a return visit with Lauren, we told him how she had been throwing tantrums and running away from us in public. He immediately pulled out his prescription pad and began talking to us about Ritalin. I told him we weren't interested in drugs. In fact, the same man had told us on a previous visit that, in her tantrums, Lauren was acting more like a typical two-year-old than when she was quiet and in her own little world. So, I was just celebrating the fact that she was coming out of her shell even more! I think it was at this visit that we decided to no longer see the doctor. He agreed that if we didn't require medical intervention at the time, our money was better spent elsewhere.

The autumn before Lauren turned three, a submission to the local Autism Society of America chapter newsletter passed before my eyes. (I was editor of the newsletter at the time.) It was a notice seeking participants for a study on the effects of chiropractic care on children with autism. Andrew, a student at the local chiropractic college was conducting the study as his thesis. I spoke to Andrew (who liked to be called Dru) on the phone about publishing the notice and we soon learned a little about each other. When Dru heard Lauren had autism, he encouraged me to have her participate in the study. I doubted that would ever happen, as Lauren had begun fighting us at doctors' offices. I couldn't picture her ever sitting still for anyone to manipulate her spine. But Craig and I attended the presentation Dru and his fellow students/researchers put on for the parents whose interest was piqued by the newsletter ad.

We didn't know much about chiropractic care. Dru explained that this study would specifically address the effects of moving only the atlas. The atlas is the bone at the top of the spine that all of the spinal column nerves pass through to go to the brain. We learned that it's important for this bone to be aligned properly, as any misalignment puts pressure on some nerves that pass through it. Even slight pressure on these nerves can have an ill effect on the body's health. I don't know if Craig and I believed everything that was said at this presentation, but Dru knew what it would take for us to have Lauren participate. He told us three things. First, the pressure that would be put on Lauren's atlas was very light. (We felt the "click" of the instrument he would use, but on our fingers.) Second, he would do anything necessary to help Lauren be comfortable throughout the study. (We were particularly worried about the x-rays and physical exam required at the beginning of the study.) Lastly, if we wanted to withdraw from the study at any time, we could. We also knew participation was free (free therapy is hard to come by) and the location of the college was close to our house, so there was no great burden on our family to participate. We signed Lauren up. Having just turned three, she was the youngest participant in the study.

There were a number of chiropractic students assigned to the various children participating in the study. Lauren's chiropractor was Dru, for which I was grateful, as he is one of the kindest, most gentle-spirited men our family has known. He also had a great sense of humor. (I'll never forget when Bryn told him my birthday was coming up on Thursday. "She's going to be 30!" she announced as though it were

100. On Lauren's Thursday visit, Dru handed me an envelope. Inside was a sympathy card, plainly signed "Dru." He got away with this only because he was slightly older than me.)

Before Lauren began seeing Dru (December 1994), she was in the pediatrician's office for sinus infections, ear infections or urinary tract infections every few weeks. She was frequently taking antibiotics. Upon beginning to receive chiropractic care, Lauren's sick visits to the doctor decreased to two per year. Lauren began interacting more in therapy and school activities. It amazed me how much better Lauren's day could be when she began it healthy. When the college study ended, Dru gave me the name of a local family chiropractor in private practice. Lauren began seeing Dr. Beth when she was four years old and still sees her on a regular basis. So does the rest of our family, as we've each discovered healing for some of our own ailments in her office. Dr. Beth has been one of our greatest assets in Lauren's healthcare, advising us whenever she hears of anything that might benefit Lauren and our family. Like many of the professionals in Lauren's life, Dr. Beth has also become a lifelong friend.

During the spring when Lauren was six years old (March 1998), we took her to Dr. Henry, a kinesiologist. Kinesiologists use muscle testing to determine what illness or allergies are weakening the body. I would describe what Dr. Henry did in his office, but Craig loves to tell people that "he danced around wearing a mask and shaking rattles" because "it's easier to believe!" His diagnosis was that Lauren was allergic to dairy products, molds and mildew and had problems with yeast overgrowth. In fact, these were the problems we suspected in Lauren (but hadn't told the doctor) so we were quite impressed. (Though, to be fair to the scientific process, I must add that these are common problems for many children with autism. In other words, the doctor could have guessed that these were Lauren's problems without ever seeing her, based on her diagnosis. Having said that, Craig and I do believe in the validity of his methods.) The doctor also declared that Lauren had digestive difficulties. Lab test results confirmed all of these diagnoses. One of Lauren's digestive problems was a parasite that thrives in unhealthy intestines.[19]

The foremost consequence of seeing Dr. Henry was the removal of dairy products from our family's diet. Lauren didn't drink milk because we already associated milk with ear infections. However, she loved pizza, nachos with melted cheese on top and Mom's homemade macaroni and cheese. These are things our whole family misses. (We sneak the pizza and nachos from time to time, but macaroni and cheese isn't something you pull out of the oven if the whole family can't sit and enjoy it.) I substituted rice milk for all our homemade baked goods recipes and made sure there was never any (visible) ice cream in the freezer to tempt Lauren. The fruit of this deprivation was evident almost immediately. Within one month, Lauren was sleeping all night! Before this, Lauren was often awake at about 3:00 A.M., sometimes sobbing as though in pain. I can't express enough how important a change this was to our family life. Craig and I finally were able to sleep seven hours straight most nights. Our dispositions (including Lauren's) were so much happier during the day, probably just because we'd redis-covered R.E.M. sleep!

Because of Lauren's mold and mildew problems, Craig and I also quickly addressed an obvious moisture problem in our family room. The carpet became saturated when it rained. A drainage problem had rotted parts of the outer wall, so water seeped into the room. Renova-tions took three months and left us with a much prettier house. More importantly, Lauren was a happier child. This may have been a direct result of the "summer of supplements" we had just completed. Lauren took oral syringes full of juice or water mixed with a variety of supple-ments throughout the day. Craig and I needed to refer to a spreadsheet that laid out dosages and frequency every time it was "time for Lauren's medicine"—there were too great a variety of gradations and frequen-cies to keep track otherwise. The effort was worth it. After completing her regimen, Lauren's digestive tract was healthier—she almost imme-diately gained weight. A friend who had babysat Lauren as a toddler used to comment on her skinny little arms and legs when she would change her diaper. She saw Lauren that fall and couldn't believe her eyes. Everyone was amazed by her new pudgy build and the obvious improvement in her health. Other gains were a happier disposition and a new interest in people and activities. For example, Lauren raked leaves and rode a bicycle that fall! Dad assisted hand over hand, of course, but Lauren initiated each activity. She independently picked up the rake and started pulling it; and she surprised us all when she stood the bike up and struggled to get onto it. When help appeared and her efforts were met with success, Lauren's obvious glee was that of any young child sharing in these activities for the first time. Her joy was contagious. I remember that October like it was a month-long celebration.

Sometime during the following year, Craig and I became aware of another of Lauren's food intolerances. She consistently became sick after eating soy products. She loved some tofu-filled Chinese dumplings at the time, so it was another sad goodbye to a few favorite foods, but having her not in pain after a meal was certainly worth it.

About a year later (Spring 1999), when Lauren was seven, Dr. Beth gave me an article to read about a boy with autism who was greatly helped by gluten and casein (dairy) being removed from his diet. I knew before receiving this article that removing gluten was something we should try, as many children who respond positively to the removal of casein tend also to respond positively to the removal of gluten. However, as always, I was waiting for the divine prompt—the sign that the time was ripe and that I was ready. I considered the article and the extensive reading I followed it up with to be my divine prompt.

Gluten is something in wheat and other grains that combines with yeast during bread-making and helps the dough to rise. All baked items on regular store shelves have gluten in them because they all have wheat flour in them (or some "enriched" derivative of wheat flour). Many packaged foods that you wouldn't think have wheat in them do have gluten in them. Believe it or not, when I decided our family was going to go gluten-free, I had been grinding my own wheat and baking all my family's bread for a year. Freshly ground whole wheat bread was a staple in our diets. So this was quite a big decision and transition for our family, but we did it.

According to the information I had read, gluten may take up to nine months to fully clear out of the body, so I was determined to try this diet for at least a year to be sure we gave it a fair chance. The first week Lauren was off gluten, she improved in so many ways, it's hard to recount them all. She started throwing and catching a ball for the first time. She started showing interest in books. She was generally calmer and more attentive. She picked up markers and drew with them for the first time. Within a month, she began drinking out of a straw. These are only a few of the changes we saw in her. Needless to say, we decided pretty quickly to stay on the diet past one year. Though there has been no continuing pattern of dramatic changes in Lauren since that first month, we continue to recognize that she is a calmer and happier child than she was before the diet.

***If interested in more detail, see Appendix B: *Going Gluten-Free*, at the end of this book.

Not long after going gluten-free (in May 1999), we took Lauren to a registered nurse named Milly, who has a business doing BioEnergetic Assessment (BEA). We discovered Milly upon beginning a new educational program with Lauren. At her first evaluation, where the professionals initially set up her program, the evaluator was also a mom of a son with autism. I spoke to her at length about Lauren's behavior and how it's directly affected by yeast. At the time, we had Lauren on acidophilus, a pro-biotic, but she still had signs of yeast infection often. This mom gave me the name and number of Milly, who had helped her son overcome his systemic yeast problems.

Milly's assessment of Lauren was probably the easiest, most pleasant medical experience we've ever had with Lauren. Milly's peaceful demeanor helped Lauren to stay calm in the room and come back to the chair over and over again after small breaks. Lauren consistently picked up the small metal rod she needed to hold for the test, while at the same time allowing Milly to hold and touch her hand in the way necessary. In the end, we had a nice readout of Lauren's level of tolerance for different substances. These readings confirmed the findings of Dr. Henry, whom we had seen over a year earlier.

By way of a completely different avenue (or so it seemed to us) Milly and Dr. Henry had come to the same conclusions about Lauren's health. Milly gave us supplements to address Lauren's yeast difficulties and advised us to keep her away from the other substances to which she had found Lauren sensitive. Most of these substances had already been removed from Lauren's diet, but now we were even more motivated to be sure her diet and environment were as needed to allow her the greatest chance to thrive. The supplement immediately seemed to help Lauren. We are very pleased with Milly, particularly as she's another fountain of knowledge about a variety of alternative healthcare practices.

Interestingly, Milly's BEA of Lauren showed that Lauren tolerates brown rice very well, but has a low tolerance for white rice. "Why would that be?" I asked Milly. "What's the difference?"

"White rice is bleached," she answered. "It's the chemical residue from the bleaching process that she is sensitive to." Ahhhh…a light bulb went on in my head. Lauren hadn't been able to go to the pool to swim all year because the water made her sick. She doesn't just experience skin contact, she also drinks it. Despite Mom's and Dad's attempts to dissuade, she guzzles mouthfuls and always throws up in the car on the way home. After going to the pool just once, her behavior is uncontrollable for two weeks afterward. Craig and I had come to the conclusion that it was the chlorine that was doing this to her, and chlorine is what they use to bleach products, even food products, like rice. More affirmation.

When Lauren was nine (Spring 2001), we were experiencing bout after bout of aggressive behavior from her. She is like a completely different child during such bouts. She can be so loving and gentle at times, and so out of control and angry in an instant. I had another nagging thought. Somewhere in my past I'd heard of the Feingold Diet, which involves removing all artificial flavorings and colorings from the child's diet. I knew it as a diet that helps many children with hyperactivity and ADD. Certainly my child is often hyper and has a severe attention problem, but I haven't yet encountered any parents of children with autism who are on the diet. The thought of it kept tugging at the back of my brain. One day, again in the spring (wellspring of new ideas or renewed energy to *try* old ideas?) I purchased a *Living Without* magazine at our local health food market. The magazine addresses issues pertinent to people on limited diets, particularly gluten-free diets. Inside this issue was an article written by a mom of a child who had begun the Feingold diet. She described one of the child's pre-diet tantrums and I sat up straight while reading it; it reminded me so much of a Lauren tantrum. Though this mom's child was verbal and said some hateful things during his outburst, his verbal expressions seemed perfectly to fit Lauren's "tone" during a tantrum. I considered it another piece of divine timing (i.e. I was ready, willing and able) so I went to the Feingold web site and soon ordered the materials necessary to start the diet. (Actually, you can start it without the materials, but I'm a little obsessive and require possessing, at my fingertips, answers to every question I might ask before engaging in anything new.) The materials, and subsequent newsletters, provide much encouragement for implementing the diet in a world where most foods readily available and most popular (especially among children) are loaded with artificial ingredients.

For our family, this was the easiest diet restriction we took on. After all, when you're gluten, casein, soy and yeast-free, you're already making most items from scratch to meet your needs. Even if you've found prepared foods that fit the bill, they're likely additive-free because they were found at a health food store. We primarily had to take only two condiments out of Lauren's diet—Heinz ketchup and Log Cabin pancake syrup. We quickly realized, however, that healthier ketchup tastes just as good as name brand, and that medium amber pure maple syrup even meets the taste requirements of Mom. (I was the Log Cabin lover.) Lauren's behavior seemed improved, but we did some tests to make sure. There was an obvious and immediate correlation between Lauren's consumption of artificial ingredients and her lack of self control. No more tests, she's staying on the Feingold Diet.

One of the greatest breakthroughs in Lauren's health, disposition and attentiveness can only be attributed to supplements. In late spring of 2001, we began using SuperNuthera, the multivitamin supplement formulated specifically for children with autism that has proper proportions of B6 and Magnesium.[20] We also began giving Lauren a different pro-biotic than she had been receiving. This is a formula made up of many different strains of bacteria, all of which are important for proper digestion. (I didn't investigate this one. It just happened to be listed on the same order form I used to get the SuperNuthera. I tried it for the purpose of saving me a twenty-six mile drive to get our usual supplement from Milly. What proper parental motivation! But if it worked as well…what a time and energy savings.) These supplements are expensive, but we began them because Lauren was, once again, frequently agitated and we were looking for help. The week she began taking these supplements, Lauren frequently played calmly and began "reading" a variety of books often. She was suddenly less interested in sitting in front of TV videos. She became more interactive, silly (like her "old self," before any aggression ever occurred) and communicative. We are so pleased! I've heard, "Wow! We have our little girl back!" come out of the mouths of Craig, Bryn and me during completely different interactions. I thank God and I keep praying that He will continue to place Craig's and my feet on the narrow and unpredictable path toward Lauren's healing.

As I write this chapter, Lauren's behavior has continued to be consistently pleasant, she's been easy to engage and she's talking much more. The only exception has been when she's on an antibiotic. Lauren has gotten thrush, a yeast infection of the mouth, each of the two times she's taken a powder oral antibiotic (which we mix with juice, but the powder residue still sits in the crevices of her mouth). Symptoms of thrush include swollen, broken and painful lips. The first time Lauren experienced it, the symptoms went away immediately upon discontinuing the antibiotic. The second incident was more severe, so I took her to the pediatrician. Lauren's regular doctor was not in. The doctor we saw said, "It's not thrush. Only infants and people with compromised immune systems get thrush."[21] Yes, well, Lauren also had parasites that only people with compromised digestive tracts tend to get. An alternative practitioner found that out for us. How can any doctor tell me my daughter doesn't have a compromised immune system when he can't tell me what autism is or what causes it? It seems to me that developing a serious disability of unknown origin while being exposed to the exact conditions as a sister who is unaffected could be evidence of a compromised immune system. My theories about Lauren's health have been dismissed many times by doctors with "Oh, that only shows up in people with compromised immune systems." What can be more compromising than something strong enough to eliminate speech and sociability and to cause self-abuse? When I "grrr" in frustration, Craig kindly reminds me to "Be patient with doctors, Honey. Remember, they're only practicing."

Though these might not fall under everyone's definition of alternative medicine or even therapy, I want to include two more success stories here. The first has to do with sleep, so it ties into the success story about Lauren's sleep improving. While removing dairy from her diet allowed Lauren to sleep through the night, she was still unsuccessful at putting herself to sleep at any regular hour or in any regular way. Craig and I had tried to keep her in her room at night, but we just ended up hating our nights. At the end of the day, which was supposed to be our time together, one of us was with Lauren in her room while the other fell asleep on the sofa trying to be quiet. We accomplished nothing in the evenings, spent no enjoyable time together and still none of us got any decent sleep. This problem came up at a program evaluation when Lauren was seven. The evaluator suggested something that many parents had tried with success. He told us to completely block out the light to Lauren's room. This would give her overactive mind nothing to focus on (or be distracted/agitated by) and would allow her to go to sleep. We couldn't put curtains or any window covering on Lauren's window, as she had torn down two sets already. In this case, the suggestion was to spray paint the window black. That weekend, Craig bought a can of navy blue spray paint and painted the outside of Lauren's bedroom window. During the day, it gave the room a mellow glow with the sunlight behind it. At night, it prevented the light from street lamps, the neighbor's carport and the moon from shining in. We put a blanket at the base of the door outside the room and the room was pitch black. Craig and I took turns lying down with Lauren and we couldn't see a thing.

Lauren began falling asleep very quickly after we said our goodnights and lay down with her. She finally had a bedtime! After a few months of Craig's or my being in the room with her, one night I suggested Bryn go to bed at the same time. (They shared the room at the time, but Bryn was in the habit of going to bed later than Lauren. Bryn regularly woke up Mom or Dad, whoever had fallen asleep with Lauren, upon coming in to go to bed.) Bryn sang lullabies to her sister, who easily fell asleep to the sweet sounds, and a new night-time routine was born. Craig, Bryn and I began taking turns putting Lauren to bed, though, Bryn often asked if she could do it because she enjoyed singing her repertoire of memorized lullabies before falling asleep. One evening, my parents were visiting from out of state and I wanted to visit with them rather than lie down with Lauren at 9:00. We went through our routine of video, using the toilet and brushing her teeth, but this time when Lauren bounded into bed and pulled the covers over her head, I didn't join her. I said our prayer, kissed her goodnight, told her I would check on her to be sure she was OK, then I left and closed the door behind me. Lauren was asleep in minutes. I did the same thing the next night, and the next, and, once again, a new routine was born. I thought I was being selfish not lying down with her so I could visit with my parents, but perhaps Lauren was glad to finally have her space back.

In our defense, Craig and I stayed with Lauren in order to keep her from getting out of bed to turn on her overhead light full blast. The light had a dimmer switch with a separate toggle to control brightness, but at this point, Lauren had figured out the tiny toggle. Would you believe it took us months to figure something else out…she can't turn the light on if there are no bulbs in the light fixture! Again, in our defense, this would have left her room pretty somber and useless during the day when her window was painted. It was only after we removed the paint from her window (while trying to sell our house) that we resorted to taking the bulbs out. It works! Natural light really does let you know when to sleep and when to wake.

Melatonin is a hormone produced by our bodies that is supposed to tell us it's time to sleep. Melatonin is also available for purchase as a supplement, which some parents have reported using to help their children with autism finally get some sleep. We tried it once for a few nights and it wasn't helpful at all. Lauren seemed to become more hyper after taking it and three hours later she might finally be asleep. I have a friend whose daughter was taking melatonin forty-five minutes before bedtime and it was very helpful. I asked my friend, "Does your daughter stay awake because she's not tired, or is she tired and just fighting sleep with every ounce of strength she can muster?" My friend looked at me as though she didn't understand the question, so I guessed that she hadn't experienced what we were experiencing with Lauren. The later it became, the harder she would try to stay awake. Even in front of a favorite, calming video, if Lauren felt her eyelids droop, she would jump up and run around in circles in order to keep awake. I remember observing this and saying to Craig, "It's as though sleep is this great abyss that she's afraid of falling into and she's fighting to stay alive." I wondered as I was saying this if sleep resembled the state of self-isolation she was more deeply in as a toddler. (We try so hard to keep her with us during the day, and she enjoys us, then we ask her to submit to the feeling at night.) I'll probably never know.

Sound therapy is another controversial activity many families have undertaken to help their children with autism. Many have shared success stories with me. Some who have paid the cost of the Berard or Tomatis methods have shared their doubts. Having myself experienced many changes in Lauren's behavior seeming to have no correlation to any therapy, I can understand why parents question what to credit for their children's improvement or regression. Craig and I have opted not to pursue any formal sound therapy, because no matter how much I read about it, I still don't comprehend the premise of its success. (I don't accept, "Just trust us, you'll see results" as a reason to put Lauren through a therapy.) I do understand that my child has very sensitive hearing and has been intolerant of many noises that most people can assign to the background. It makes sense to me that if I expose my child to the sound frequencies that frustrate or hurt her in a regular, non-intrusive way, she will likely become desensitized to these frequencies. That's exactly what we have done and that's exactly what we believe has happened.

I've mentioned playing music often in other chapters of this book, but I want to make clear that Craig and I believe this has been very important to Lauren's success over the years. For the price of about twenty CD's that our family enjoys owning and listening to anyway, we have accumulated a method of therapy far cheaper than what any other therapy costs. What I didn't mention in the other chapters (because it is most recent in Lauren's "musical history") is that Lauren now enjoys listening to a variety of music, including the radio, and becomes bored when the style of music remains the same for too long. As a toddler, Lauren tolerated only Bach, Mozart and a few contemporary piano styles. Over the years, we have increased her classical repertoire and introduced blues, rock and country. Today, she loves listening to the unpredictable radio in the car and even at home. She doesn't even mind most commercials. (Though I mute it when anyone starts screaming an ad at me. Why would I ever give someone my money when they've just hurt my eardrums?!) At home, we used to have to play one CD at a time and be aware of when the CD ended and a new one began, as Lauren's mood could change drastically. Sometimes, she even walked us to the stereo and asked us to change the music. Today, Lauren prefers a variety of artists with somewhat similar styles. We can now put five of our favorite CD's into the player, set it to play randomly, and enjoy hours of a variety of music as a family. Perhaps Lauren has just matured in her musical tastes as she has aged, but she hasn't matured as noticeably in many other matters of development. She also doesn't react violently when children scream, trains go by or loud machines sound. I feel certain that her purposeful exposure to a variety of "sounds of life" has well prepared her brain for the occasional extremes. Now she remains calm when she hears such sounds, instead of reacting like she's being physically assaulted. That's worth the price of any therapy.[22]

Toilet Training

This chapter is specifically for parents who can't imagine how they will ever toilet train their son or daughter with autism. I was there once and I wished so much that someone would come along and lead me through the steps. If your child is more inclined than Lauren was to use the toilet, maybe you don't need this chapter. If not, maybe something in our experience will be of help.

About the time Lauren was turning seven years old, Craig and I decided it was time to toilet train her. Books on the subject advise parents to wait until a child shows signs of readiness, such as an interest in sitting on the toilet or an ability to hold it for a long time. Lauren showed no sign of readiness. She was perfectly content to continue wearing pull-up diapers, possibly for a very long time. But the only pull-up diapers that fit her were very expensive (I figured out that we were paying over $250.00 per month for diapering supplies) and she was outgrowing the largest size they sold anyway. (Since then, a larger size has come out on the market—same price but fewer in the package, of course.)

Important to mention before I go into the process of training are some strategies we implemented to keep our family as happy as possible during the process. First of all, Craig took a week off from work. We knew this would be a full-time effort that would wipe me out if I did it alone. We foresaw the cleaning that would need to be done after accidents while vigilance in Lauren's care and training would still need to be maintained. I don't know if we believed one week would be anywhere near enough, but our other plans suggested we weren't so confident. I wrote a letter to all our local friends to let them know what we were undertaking. (By the end of this book, you'll realize I'm a big fan of seeking my community of friends' support. Our family has many loving friends who desire to help. Even though I'm a pretty independent person, I realize that I enjoy meeting others' needs when I can. The times that I've gone to the extreme of asking for help, I've felt the push come from outside of myself. The love of these people is substantial. It draws me to reach out for it and to touch it rather than allow myself to be overcome by life's challenges. Lauren has allowed me to know the love of friendship the way it's portrayed in the movies—when you walk out of the theater crying.)

I knew we would have to stay close to home throughout the training process, as there was no way Lauren could be trained using public restrooms. The only place Lauren went at the time was to her speech and occupational therapy sessions. I asked our friends for three favors with the letter that follows:

Hi friends!

This Wednesday is Lauren's 7th birthday, and to "mark" the occasion, Nannette and Craig are forcing Lauren to toilet train. (Actually, the fact that she has outgrown the largest size disposable pants available in stores is also a factor in the timing.) This means there will be no more disposable pants in the house and Mom, Dad or someone will have to be continuously at Lauren's side to take her to the bathroom (on a schedule and as needed), to guide her through the steps, and to clean up any accidents.

Why am I telling you this? Well, over the years, many close friends have realized how challenging life with Lauren can be and have asked how they could help. Typically, we just say, "Pray for Lauren, please—specifically, that she talks." Though prayer is still our number one need—specifically that Lauren accepts and learns this toileting thing quickly—we will also be challenged by the simplest everyday tasks for awhile. So, we can think of some very tangible ways that we would love some help.

We will be pretty much homebound until Lauren shows some mastery of toileting. It may take 3 days; it may take many months. (Pray for 3 days!) During this time, it will be extremely difficult to run basic errands. So those who can, I ask that if you are headed to the grocery store, and you'll be seeing one of us soon or have time to drop off some groceries, please call us and ask if we need anything. (We'll try to keep our grocery money in cash so we can pay you right back.) Also, please think of us if you are headed to any of our other basic errand places: Target, CVS, Petsmart or post office, for example. (If you call us just as we've run out of toothpaste or light bulbs, you will be a saint in our book!)

Also, if you or your family is headed out somewhere fun and it wouldn't be a bother to have another kid aboard, please consider calling and inviting Bryn to join you. (Even if it's just the mall. She hasn't been to one in 2 years.) We won't be able to take her anywhere for awhile and I'm sure she'll be thrilled at every opportunity to escape our preoccupied household.

I know some of our friends won't be able to help in these ways, so remember that our first request is for prayer. We love you, and thank you for all the caring ways you've been in our lives over the last few years. And thank you in advance for whatever way you're able to help.

We'll let you know when everyone's using the potty successfully and we're out and about again!

Love,

Nannette & Craig

(I put our phone number here.)

The most important part of this letter to me was the opportunity it would hopefully present for Bryn to get away. I didn't want this period of her life (if it turned out to be lengthy) to leave her with legitimate reason to complain about her childhood. There was no fear of that when all was said and done. Bryn was invited to: the mall; an open house at the new local Major League Baseball stadium; a Renaissance festival; and to friends' houses to play often. She has very little memory of Lauren's toilet training.

The outer preparations having been made, we decided on a toilet training strategy. Just like Bryn did when she was toilet training as a toddler, we knew Lauren had to be bare-bottomed during the process, as underwear feel too much like diapers. But Bryn wore dresses while training. Lauren had been refusing to wear dresses for over a year. As soon as I pulled one over her head, she fought to pull it back off. (My theory is that she realized Mom dressed her in pants and shorts when staying at home, but put her in a dress whenever we were going someplace "special," such as yet another doctor's office. I didn't blame her for avoiding that trap!) Pants and shorts were out, as they provide a thickness like a diaper. I didn't want her to run around naked, so I knew a reintroduction to dresses was the first battle.

This battle was actually the shortest of any we have undergone with Lauren. I went to the store and bought the most comfortable pullover all cotton dresses I could find. After Lauren's bath on Day One, I lovingly and happily talked about the beautiful dress she was going to wear that day. I pulled it over her head and she almost immediately began struggling to pull it off. I lost the sing-songy voice, pulled the dress back down firmly and said in a loud and stern voice, "Leave the dress on!" Lauren left the dress on and began wearing dresses more than any other type of garment from that day forward. I know…this is not a technique in any parenting books. If it were, it would probably be called "Compliance by means of fear that Mommy's head will begin to spin." I have never used this method with any success on any day following this incident, so I can't recommend it, but it worked this time. (Thank you, God! I had nothing else up my sleeve.)

Beyond her remaining bare-bottomed, the plan was to take Lauren to the bathroom frequently on a schedule and to be vigilant for any sign that she needed to go, so that we could "catch her" when she had the urge. This is pretty much the way you train a typical child, but most children I know won't let the urine spew onto the hardwood floor with seemingly no sense of this being a problem. (Most will at least hide.) Lauren's version of hiding was to sit on someone's lap, as though she wanted to give them a big hug, then to "make herself more comfortable." Needless to say, this "natural" form of toilet-training took a turn onto a more forced route pretty quickly. It had to; Craig had taken a week off from work for this adventure. We didn't realize until we were a few days into it that we had been overly confident. We believed we'd see some sign of understanding within the week that the bathroom was the direction to head in when the urge struck, but there was no such understanding apparent.

Early in the week, we began taking books into the bathroom and trying to have Lauren spend long periods of time in there, so we were closer to the toilet when it was needed. For ourselves, there was a little box-shaped chair to sit on across from the toilet in the tiny bathroom. When Lauren did sit on the toilet, she could hold onto us or lay her head in our laps. We would rub her back to help her get comfortable, but she would consistently pop up when she felt finished with the activity, as though to say, "That was a pleasant time, let's go do something else now." Don't get me wrong. She peed in the bathroom. She peed in the bathtub, she peed on our laps and she peed onto towels, but she wouldn't pee into the toilet.

We showed Lauren books for children about using the toilet. Of course, she rarely looked directly at the pictures in them. To try to get her to remember the proper place to put her pee, I came up with a song/poem that I said to her frequently when I thought she might soon be "forgetful":

> *We hold our pee pee in our body*
> *Till we're sitting on the potty.*

When this seemed to help her keep her legs crossed at a later point in training, I added:

> *We hold our poopy in our body*
> *Till we're sitting on the potty.*

On the Saturday before Craig went back to work, I was turning into a mean person. I guess I wasn't overtly obnoxious, though, as Craig simply complimented me on being so "determined" when I tried the only thing left I knew to do. I took Lauren into the bathroom with a cup of water and some favorite books. (Her favorites were books with shiny surfaces and textures she could stim on, but I thought the end justified the means this time.) Then I had her sit on the toilet until she used it. Sounds so simple, doesn't it? It took almost two hours before she peed the first time. In that time, she and I looked at books relatively calmly for about one-third of the time. I held her firmly (with every ounce of strength) while she screamed and fought to get up (with every ounce of strength) about one-third of the time. And I just kept my hands on her ready for the next battle about one-third of the time. I spoke to her lovingly and as calmly as possible throughout. Even when she was justifiably angry, I talked to her about what I needed her to do, how I knew it was hard and how I was not letting her up until she did it.

When I finally heard a steady stream of liquid hitting the toilet water, I was in a state of disbelief. Craig experienced the same surreal feeling the first time he heard it. We each couldn't have been more moved if Bach himself (my favorite) had left his grave for a few minutes to play us a concerto on an ancient harpsichord. The sound of a child being successful years beyond the time most children experience such success—it's music to the ears, even when it's about a basic bodily function.

Upon leaving the bathroom, I announced Lauren's success to the rest of the family. (The trick with any accomplishment is to be excited without frightening her with our excitement. We wouldn't want her to avoid the toilet in order to avoid our overwhelming cheers and praises. We're pretty practiced around here in praising no louder than a regular speaking tone.) At last, Craig was able to unveil our final coup. He had bought helium balloons and a helium tank to use at home. As he praised Lauren for her success, Craig blew up a balloon. Lauren's eyes were wide and she was shaking with excitement as he handed her her favorite toy. (Daddy must have seemed like a hero to her. Never before had she found this toy outside special places away from home.) We called both grandmas to brag, which we hoped held significance to Lauren despite the fact that she never spoke on the phone or wanted it near her ear. We hoped the reason behind the celebration was understood.

I'm pretty sure the reason was understood, as we had to go right back into the bathroom even before Lauren was ready to let go of the balloon. This time, it took forty-five minutes of holding Lauren on the toilet before she went again. The party was as big when we came out of the bathroom this time. We were making obvious progress. In fact, the next time I took her into the bathroom, Lauren immediately peed in the potty. From that point forward, she understood the purpose of the toilet. In three hours, we had accomplished through a forced teaching process what I had foreseen taking weeks or months. Chalk one up to a mom getting discouraged and taking the bull by the horns (or the child by the arms) and not letting go.

The biggest problem during Lauren's toilet training was that she had no idea what to do with a bowel movement. In the first week of being bare-bottomed, she didn't seem to know what to do with that urge, so she held it in. She held it in for days. We would find smears of feces on the floor, blankets and pieces of furniture. When it did finally come out, it was not into the toilet. After she learned to pee in the toilet, we knew the next battle was the bowel movement. Lauren could hold it for days, but Craig, Bryn and I began to recognize the "poopy dance." She would hang onto a chair or table, bend at the waist, twist her body and cross her legs. As soon as one of us would see this, Craig or I would take her into the bathroom to hold her on the toilet until something came out or until the urge had definitely subsided. (After a few hours, someone has to give in.) About a month after starting this process, Lauren put her first bowel movement into the toilet. It was another cause for celebration. We had saved helium and balloons for the occasion. She had a few accidents after this incident, but she pretty consistently used the toilet for its intended purpose from that point on. (Well, there was the occasional fishing-for-toys expedition, but she mostly used it for what it was intended.)

I must admit to one miscalculation we experienced right at the start of toilet training. We had cockily vowed we would never have disposable panties in the house again. Lauren would have to forego wearing a panty at night because we believed that if we allowed her to wet in a panty any part of the day, she would be more confused about the process. The first night, we had her out of her bed about three times so we could change sheets. Lauren had a very hard time going to sleep at the time, so it was a miserable night. The second night was similar. I broached the compromise with Craig the next day. He said, "I'm so relieved you said it. I was thinking we'd never get any sleep if we didn't give in." We began concentrating on training Lauren during the day and decided to night-train her after we had success during the day.

To this day, we're still working on night-training. Lauren is refusing to wear the pull-up diaper at night, so we have our natural push to night-train. But she's also now going to bed on her own and sleeping peacefully through the night. It would have been difficult (perhaps impossible) to night-train when she was such a bad sleeper. Each time Lauren wakes up dry and the bed is dry, it feels like we've reached a little milestone. Other milestones that we anticipated nervously, then celebrated, included the first time Lauren wore underwear after being trained. When I put them on her and she left them on, I wondered if she would go back to wetting herself. When she didn't, we rejoiced. The process seemed complete. Then winter came and we had to reintroduce pants. Perhaps the process never ends.

The first place Lauren used the bathroom somewhere other than her home was at her speech therapist's house. The first public bathroom was in our local grocery store. The first long distance car ride, when she held it until we were in a filthy rest area bathroom then "went" along with the rest of us—that was exciting.

My oh my, Lauren does give us many simple reasons to celebrate!

PART II
What I've Learned

○ ○

"You shall not muzzle an ox while it is treading out the corn...because the plowman should plow in hope, and the thresher in hope of receiving a share."

—1 Corinthians 9:9-10

"Drop the stimmy..."

"Drop the stimmy and put your hands up!" I don't know that any one in our family has actually said those words to Lauren, but they convey some feelings we have about staying on top of Lauren's stim toys lately. We're constantly on patrol and she knows she's guilty when she's caught, as she hands the stimmy right over.

"What in the world is a stimmy?" you may be asking. If so, this chapter is for you. I was at dinner with a friend last night and felt the need to go into a lengthy explanation of self-stimulatory behavior (self-stim). I was trying to express the difficulty of choosing to take away an item or activity that apparently gives my child so much pleasure (and keeps her occupied). I realized my friend wasn't appreciating why this was such a conundrum, so I helped her to understand. I'm pretty sure she felt quite dragged into the conundrum by the time I was done, as she seemed to appreciate what an assignment it was to stay on top of such behavior while trying to keep a peaceful household.

My explanation of self-stim will, of course, be inaccurate, simply because I don't have autism. I bother to try to explain it anyway, because I'm tired of trying to explain it from start to finish, like I tried with my friend last night. There are so many angles to look at when trying to understand this behavior that I become a little excited while talking about it. I'm trying to keep my mouth talking about one aspect of the explanation while my brain has jumped to another. It's exhausting. Perhaps from today on, I can just hand someone this chapter and say, "Here you go, this is the best explanation I can give you."

It's not only for my personal relief that I want to dedicate some pages here to self-stim. Self-stimulatory behavior is the aspect of autism that makes it stand out in a crowd. The behavior often, unfortunately, defines a child. Have you ever heard anyone say something like, "Oh yes, that boy had autism, too. He used to rock all the time and wave his hands in front of his face." Do you hear how this person's definition of autism *is* the self-stim behaviors?

Self-stim is the cause of a great deal of misunderstanding about people with autism. Should you let them do it or not let them do it? (Do you always have a choice?) If you've consistently told a child that something that stimulates her is off-limits, and she sneaks the item when you're out of the room, is she simply being defiant? No matter how many times I explain my daughter's self-stim behaviors, there are still some people who treat her as though she's a defiant beast when she continues the behavior. I'm all for parents asserting their authority and taking control of situations, but these people are usually the ones who think they should be able to dangle a stim object in front of my child and she should politely ignore it. This is the only test they will accept as proof that she's made progress.

Then there are the situations where kind people tell you, "Your child did great today! She loved splashing in the tub of water so much that we let her do it all afternoon!" I'm sure these people don't realize such activity is similar to a child without autism spending hours on end staring at a TV test pattern.

My knowledge of self-stim behavior is simply what I've garnered over the years from reading books by people with autism and professionals who work with people with autism; teaching children with autism; picking the brains of professionals I admire; and observing people with autism—particularly my daughter, of course. As I say, some of my assertions may be wrong. Certainly some won't apply to every child; we know from our discussion about the diagnosis of autism that two people with autism might have no two symptoms alike. But my thoughts have proven beneficial in helping my daughter within our family. At the least, I hope these ideas will further your own thinking about the true nature of the behavior of people with autism.

There are a few assumptions that need to be understood in a discussion of self-stim behaviors in autism.

First: There's an intelligent brain inside this person.
Second: This intelligent person wants the same basic things that every typical person wants: to be pain free, to be like others, to receive love, to feel good, to be as independent as possible, to be accepted, and to have something interesting to think about.
These first two assumptions are risky for me to make, as there are many professionals (and even parents) who think it quite important to place a number on a child, then treat the child according to that number. I have never seen any use made of an IQ score except to further limit a child's access to opportunity. For more discussion about IQ testing of people with autism, read the chapter entitled "Respect" in this book.

In case you don't know a child for whom self-stim is a significant problem, here are some examples of self-stim behaviors, some of which have been a part of our family's life: rocking; twirling around; flapping hands or arms; chewing or biting on fingers, arms or objects; pulling own hair; squinting eyes almost closed; staring at patterns, such as in busy carpets; passing fingers over objects with patterns, such as fences, chair backs or window blinds; and flicking objects. These are just a few examples of many possible self-stimulating activities. The harm in some of these activities is obvious. Others may just seem like distractions that make the child stand out in a crowd. Each of them is an expression of a need.

We know that in all people with autism, there is sensory dysfunction. Though we can't yet pinpoint the cause of this dysfunction, we know that, to some extent, the brain's interpretation of sensory perceptions is inaccurate. In other words, what comes in through the five senses is interpreted differently by this person's brain than it is by most other people's brains. For example, certain sound frequencies that are pleasant to most people may sound like fingernails on a chalkboard to a person with autism. Certain textures, such as lotion or sand, may send shivers up an autistic person's spine the way that sensing a snake circling my feet would send them up mine. (OK, I'd actually bolt if that really happened.) The smell of native foods prepared by a classmate's Vietnamese mom used to make Lauren unable to sit at the lunch table with this boy. Even if she was very hungry, she was afraid to sit anywhere near it. Of course, it didn't happen when this boy was absent or when he brought in McDonald's, so it wasn't too difficult for an astute teacher to figure out the true problem, even though Lauren was non-verbal.

Not to discredit your elementary school teachers, but when you learn about sensory dysfunction, you learn that there are actually seven senses. Besides vision, hearing, smell, taste and touch, there are the *vestibular* and *proprioceptive* senses. The vestibular system has to do with the inner ear and controls your sense of balance. The proprioceptive system is what allows your muscles to know where your body is in space and to react to that information. People with autism often have sensory difficulties with one or both of these two senses. This may have something to do with a child's rocking and spinning, or with an intense need to know her boundaries. (Even when she was a toddler, Lauren thoroughly familiarized herself with the perimeter of any new place we entered. If there was a door, she had to go through it, apparently to determine if this space continued, so she could completely map it out in her mind.) If a person is confused about her body's personal boundaries, knowing the physical boundaries of the environment may help bring some order to her chaos.

So now we know that a person with an intelligent mind and with common motivations is experiencing discomfort, perhaps even pain and fear, as a result of her body's misinterpreted perceptions. What would a non-autistic person do in this case? He would probably seek a place where he could hide out from the world to get some peace. And that's what people with autism do, too. They hide out. Of course if they found caves to hide out in, people would drag them out and say, "Come on, join this world." (Though she's never found a cave to hide in, Lauren loves closets and small spaces. We sometimes even find her just standing behind open doors in the small space between the door and the wall.) Because we insist they physically stay with us, people with autism seek solace hiding out inside their own bodies and their own minds. I'm personally impressed by an autistic person's ability to keep the world at bay despite the bombardment of color, noise and activity day-in and day-out. I can't imagine possessing that depth of concentration for any length of time.

When Lauren was a baby, she would stare at her hand for an hour at a time, sometimes seeming to trace the lines on it with her finger, ever so slowly turning it so that she had seen every cranny. Before she was diagnosed, we called her our little philosopher. In between giggling at us and acting like a normally developing child, she simply seemed to have an eye for detail and an intense interest in this appendage—this amazing creation of God. This is an example of a person shutting down to the rest of the world. Lauren especially liked to study her hand while we were traveling in the car, which was a relief to us as she was content for long periods on road trips. As the world raced past her in a blur outside her window, while the radio and car noises muffled conversation in the front seat, she was creating and enjoying her own little world that was probably a lot more peaceful than the one surrounding her at the moment.

This is what intelligent people do when limited by their circumstances. They create a reality to dwell on other than the one that surrounds them, until help arrives. This is what many P.O.W's do in prison camps. In many ways, autism is very much like a prison—one we're doing our best to help Lauren escape every moment of every day.

Self-stim is that reality a person with autism creates for herself. It's not a randomly chosen reality, but a world created out of necessity to meet some very real needs. In search of peace, a child with autism strives to meet her extreme sensory needs with the resources she has available. Perhaps she only feels where her body is in space while she's getting pressure from jumping or clapping. After a while, jumping and clapping may provide a calming predictability, as well as an outlet for pent up energy and stress, so the child is naturally rewarded and motivated to continue the behavior. This is a vicious cycle. A self-stim behavior can calm, entertain and excite a person—everything that's needed to replace that outside world that confounds and terrifies—temporarily. Like a drug, it's soon not enough to keep the outside world at bay. This intelligent person needs more to keep herself interested, while at the same time, the sensory problem is not being addressed. As in any addiction, the causal problems need to be addressed, or the person, seeking more self-stim as a temporary fix, will fall deeper into a pattern and further away from the world in which we want her to live.

I may have sounded, at first, like I was idealizing self-stim because it's the logical action of an intelligent person in a painful situation who can't convey a need for help. While I do ponder the process in awe, I also strive to eliminate it entirely from my home. I want my child wholly with me, so I can teach her things that I can't teach her while she's preoccupied with stimming.

For a long time, Lauren's most pervasive form of stimming has centered around what I believe is a desire to feel weight pulling against her body. She seeks objects that she can flick or just flop around, that bounce back, such as balloons, plastic soda bottles (preferably with soda or water still in them for the weight) and any toy that has some kind of string or rod attached. She also likes to click many plastic and metal objects against her teeth and feel them on her lips. Lauren can detect a toy or object that will fulfill this desire from across any crowded room. For many years, it was a huge battle to keep, or take away, the object from her; but her family has been perseverant. Today, she usually knows when an object is off limits, and often brings it to us to hand over before we can say, "Lauren, give me the _____." Even objects that are new to her, such as items she discovers at a friend's house, she will hand over upon request. I believe this is primarily because she understands more language and has a greater desire to obey than she had before. But I also like to think she has an appreciation for the abyss she's experienced while stimming. Though the temptation to stim is great, the joy she knows from interacting with her family and friends is greater.

One sensory difference in many people with autism which is important for parents and teachers to recognize is that the person's peripheral vision may be stronger than her central vision. Central vision is the ability to focus on one piece of visual information while not being distracted by everything else in the visual field. At an early age, normally developing people easily focus on a person's face, or a picture in a book, directly in front of them. A person with underdeveloped central vision, and stronger peripheral vision, will at the least be distracted by people walking by or the hands holding the book; at the most, she will never even see the person's face or the book because her focus is to the sides of these things. Many forms of self-stim engage this peripheral vision, thereby strengthening it, to the detriment of central vision. For example, many children with autism love to swing because there is constant, exciting movement to their sides. Many professionals encourage lots of swinging for children with autism because they love it so much, but care should be taken that while trying to engage a child, you're not actually encouraging her to get lost in a world of movement, wind and color.

OK, so I'm discouraging you from allowing children to swing. No way. Our many indoor and outdoor swings have been some of the greatest blessings in our enjoyment of Lauren. We've had swings hanging in our family room which Lauren could relax on (in her own space), or show off in, while friends or new people visited. The swing was her reason to be in the room with us. She wouldn't have been there without it. It served the purpose of introducing her to this interesting, but stressful, world of socializing just for the fun of it. Activity without obvious purpose can be stressful to many people with autism, and has certainly sometimes been for Lauren. I've also used the swing as motivation for speech:

"Lauren swing?" I ask, then wait for a word that sounds like "more" or "swing" or "again" before giving her another push.

I've used the swing to give conversation purpose(—that important *purpose* again):

"How high can you go, Lauren? As high as my hands?" She's pure excitement when she gets up higher than my hands can reach. "How do you want me to push you?" She becomes quite annoyed as she tries to convey to me exactly how her dad pushes her. You know...the "3...2...1...BLAST-OFF!" I should have known somehow. I finally get it close enough to make her happy!

Just be careful of all activities that appear to give a child a tremendous amount of pleasure. Maybe it's not self-stim. Ask yourself: Will she share this activity with someone else? Does she accept variation to the activity introduced by someone else? Can you engage her in an interaction during the activity? Does it seem that the more she gets, the more she seeks?

I've known two little boys with autism who enjoyed lining up toy cars in a row. One boy's mom was pleased that he'd taken to this activity as it was his first interest in anything that others could share. The family began teaching him to count and to name his colors using the rows of cars. They introduced games with the cars by starting a pattern of colors and number of cars and the boy would try to imitate the pattern as quickly as he could figure it out. The other boy's mom was quite distressed with her son's new interest. When I asked if maybe she could try to engage him in an interaction using the cars, she said, "Oh, no. We are not allowed near his rows, and if we touch them, he screams as though he's in pain!" What qualifies as a stim activity for one child with an autism diagnosis isn't necessarily one for another child. Like everything else in the world of autism, it takes a loving detective to figure out what's healthy for a child so choices may be made accordingly.

For our family, some stim activities are easy to stop, some are very difficult to stop, and some just go away suddenly without anyone even realizing it right away. The toy stims are easy to stop. We simply take away the toy. As I mentioned, this used to be much more difficult. Even today, a beloved balloon is something I rarely take away. I prefer to wait until Lauren's asleep then politely introduce the balloon to the scissors drawer. (Scissors are much gentler than sewing needles.)

A few years ago, Lauren had an intense interest in the heel seams of people's socks. (We all remember this as one of her cutest stims.) As soon as someone would kick off a shoe, Lauren would be at his or her feet tracing the little curved seam with a finger, practically standing on her head so she could follow the seam to its end. After about a week of this, a friend came to the house. Lauren immediately sat her down and pulled off her shoes so that she could check out her socks. (Granted, they were the first pair of rose colored socks she'd seen, and they had an interesting, deeper rosy red seam.) Though I chuckled at the time, as our friend is dear and kind, I thought, "Enough is enough," and wondered how we were going to stop this obsession. However, I don't remember a single sock seam check after the day she pulled our friend's shoes off. I don't know if she encountered an aversive natural consequence (pee-yoo!) or if she finally figured out what her inquiring mind wanted to know about sock seams, but this was a stim that mysteriously disappeared as suddenly as it appeared.

The other day, we encountered a stim that was very difficult to stop. We have (I'm almost embarrassed to admit) a plastic Santa Claus that, when plugged in, plays obnoxiously high-pitched Christmas carols while Santa's arm lowers a bubble wand into some bubble juice, then comes back up again to allow him to blow bubbles (when his blower is working properly). We place this up high so that Lauren can't touch it, but she can enjoy the bubbles floating all over the place. This year, Lauren loved this Santa Claus. While he was on, she made lots of loud noises, which I believe may have been singing, as she should recognize most of the tunes—a positive. She slapped at and twirled in the bubbles, sometimes trying to get them to pop on her mouth—iffy. She would also allow no one in the room—a definite negative. A greater negative was that when we turned Santa Claus off, she became angry and aggressive, and begged to have him turned on again. When we hid him, she fought to get him back. The rest of the day, Lauren was completely lost to us. The next day, she continued to beg for Santa, but started to bounce back. This Santa Claus episode was the impetus for my conversation about self-stim with my friend, as well as my motivation for beginning this chapter. Autism isn't just about the stim behaviors, but the behaviors and how we deal with them can make or break many days for people with autism.

Some behaviors associated with autism may not seem to fit my explanation of self-stim. Some behaviors, such as perseverative[23] talking or questioning, closing or opening all the doors or cabinets in the house, or flicking on and off light switches, may seem more like symptoms of OCD (obsessive/compulsive disorder) than a type of self-stim.

When I see Lauren doing something that doesn't obviously meet a sensory need, I ask myself, "What is she getting out of it?" Right now, Lauren requires all doors in our house to be shut. It's not much of a problem, as she's more than happy to take the time to do it herself, but we have an old house with two entry doors and a closet door in just about every room. Some days, the sound of doors closing can get to the sanest of minds. Lauren has always needed to know precisely her boundaries in any space, so maybe this is just an updated version of her need to map out and secure the perimeter of her location. As I think about it, she's taken a step forward by actually changing those boundaries and taking personal control over them. She's not angry when someone opens a door or leaves it open, but eventually, she'll realize it's open and will close it. This activity seems to serve a similar purpose as a self-stim; Lauren is increasing predictability in her surroundings, creating order out of chaos.

I don't necessarily know why Lauren does something like shutting doors all the time, and she might not know either. This may be something she did once or twice almost accidentally, got caught up in, and doesn't know how to stop. A typical person would just decide to walk away and go do something else. The ability to start, stop or transition from one activity or topic to the next is a very real physical process called motor planning. Motor planning difficulties are common in people with autism. A person with such difficulties may not have the ability to communicate from her brain to her muscles a desire to stop an activity. It could be that the person doesn't have the ability to think up or initiate a new activity, so she sticks to what she knows. Appreciating motor planning challenges may help you to help a person through these difficulties.

Sometimes it's obvious to me that Lauren wants to stop an activity, but just doesn't know how. She tends to whine and act frustrated despite the fact that she chose the activity in the first place. To help her stop this activity and transition to a new one, I think about what will give her closure. It's often just a matter of setting an obvious goal, helping her to meet that goal, and giving her motivation to move on to the next activity. In the door-closing example, I might say, "OK, Lauren, let's close all the doors in the dining room, then we'll go outside." I make sure she has whatever visual cues are necessary to our going outside, then I watch her, or help her, close the rest of the doors. I praise her for accomplishing that goal, take her hand, and walk her to where we put our shoes on, enthusiastically talking to her the whole while about going outside. (Enthusiasm is so important. Why should a person be motivated to transition to something new if even *you* aren't excited about it?)

A few years ago, I began noticing that every time Lauren walked through a doorway, she did a little twirl. If she had been taking ballet, I probably would have just brushed it off, but she wasn't taking ballet and it seemed very much like a self-stim. Concerned that this might grow to be a bigger fetish, I started making a point of announcing when we were going to move into the next room, then took her hand and didn't allow her to spin as we walked through the doorway together. I only did this when I thought of it, as she certainly moves from room to room more often than when I'm with her, but she almost immediately stopped the twirling. Whatever panic or difficulty existed in transitioning from one room to the next seemed to abate when she was prepared verbally for the transition. She was probably unaware that she even did that little dance when she learned by experience that nothing bad would happen if she didn't do it.

If you've seen the movie *Awakenings*, with Robin Williams playing Dr. Malcolm Sayer,[24] you may recall the scene where Dr. Sayer is watching a non-verbal institutionalized patient walk across the community room, but she stops partway. Dr. Sayer assumes that her goal is the water fountain at the opposite side of the room, and looks for an explanation for her inability to continue. Suddenly, the doctor realizes something—the floor the woman walked across has a black and white checkerboard pattern. During the night, Dr. Sayer uses some markers to draw a continuation of the checkerboard pattern on the rest of the floor all the way to the wall. The next day, the patient stops for a moment at the same spot on the floor, but then continues all the way to her destination. (To the doctor's surprise, she walks past the fountain and to the window next to the fountain to gaze out.) Her "purposeless" walking had a purpose. The woman had a goal, but was unable to press on toward it because a visual cue had been perceived as a boundary. Changing the visual cue was a simple remedy, but only possible because someone cared enough to work at seeing the situation from the woman's perspective.

I often think of this scene when Lauren looks down from the top of the stairs at her speech therapist's house, but her foot won't budge to take that first step down. If I try to force her, she struggles, as though I'm trying to throw her into a pit. One day, I spent a few minutes of waiting time during her therapy session trying to see that narrow stairway the way she sees it. I squatted down and squinted a little and Whoa! Those stairs suddenly appeared much steeper than I'd ever seen them. I also looked at the wall across from where Lauren would stand at the top of the stairs. After all, I know to look at the steps and concentrate on where that first foot should land, but that's not necessarily where she's looking while standing here. Whoa again! There's absolutely no floor butting against that wall anywhere in sight! If I didn't look down at the stairs (which, by the way, are the same shade as the walls, so they don't catch your eye), it certainly did look like a great abyss. Imagine feeling pushed into this before taking a second to center yourself and realizing, "OK, there's that first step."

Today, I'm sometimes smart enough to be pre-emptive about that first step. As she's walking toward the stairs, I say something like, "OK, Lauren, let's go down the stairs. Here's the first step," while motioning so that her eyes follow my hand downward. That's usually all it takes to help her make the transition.

I attribute many of Lauren's difficult-to-explain behaviors to a fear or anxiety that I simply can't imagine because I've never experienced such anxiety. Lauren avoids pointing to or touching an item directly in order to request it. For example, if she wants orange juice, she will hold my arm, guide it to the orange juice carton and set my hand on it. If she wants the television on, she takes someone's hand, walks up to the television, throws the person's hand at it, then sits down to await her show. Though Lauren first learned to point with a finger a few years ago, she tends to touch pictures of objects to make requests with other body parts instead, using her forehead to tap a picture, for example. I believe this is a way for Lauren to avoid taking "personal responsibility" for her actions. She seems to have a fear of revealing her "will"—that which makes her who she is as a unique individual. It's as though Lauren fears physical pain from her mind being revealed—the same type of pain or discomfort she experiences from her unique perceptions of more tangible things, like sights, sounds and physical touch. Donna Williams[25] writes about this phenomenon in her books. I specifically remember her telling about the anxiety of being at a dinner table with people she liked very much. She wanted to be able to interact with them, but the emotions surrounding the fact that they were all gathered together made her virtually speechless. She wanted to reveal herself and her emotions to her friends in conversation, but the anxiety involved prevented her.

Emotions do the same thing to Lauren. She seeks physical touch from people she enjoys, but it usually lasts only a few moments before she's off in a corner, squinting her eyes to cut down on whatever visual information is adding to the chaos the emotions have produced. Sometimes, after a particularly loving moment, Lauren will turn on me like a cat that has been petted for half a minute too long. It's as though the emotion involved turns into a monster—a monster frightening enough that Lauren will turn to fight it (me) or she will run away from it to stim in some corner in an attempt to regain a sense of order.

I sometimes have an experience at night that helps me to empathize with Lauren. When I'm very stressed or thinking about many things while trying to go to sleep, my thoughts will suddenly turn into an image that is as much feeling as it is visual. The best I can describe the visual is that there are too many shapes and colors to count and they're all mangled into a heap, too complexly convoluted to ever be untangled. I know this feeling/picture intimately and when it appears, I startle out of my half-asleep stupor and am afraid to close my eyes again. I must remain fully awake for a minute or so and have my thoughts or emotions calmed or better sorted before I close my eyes again, or the "monster" will soon reappear. I hope revealing her will (her "self") and her deepest emotions isn't as disturbing to Lauren as my night-time "monster" is to me. If it is, I don't blame her in the least for wanting to avoid any revelation of her self—even the part of the self that is just interested in obtaining a cup of orange juice. (But I still insist she use her own finger to point to orange juice, pictures, and other items.)

Though behaviors caused by motor planning and anxiety difficulties may not be self-stim, I include them here because they're often viewed as just more bizarre behavior. Understanding the purpose of behavior is the key to helping a person change it, if desired. Sometimes the purpose is elusive, so it's good to have several theories in your pocket as you try to help.

Taking away stim toys is one way to stop a stim that includes an object, but there are many other types of stim that can be much more perplexing to figure out and to replace. We know that the stim expresses a need, so we seek to meet that need in more appropriate ways. For example, if a child is chewing on her hands or other surfaces, she may have an oral pain or other physical need. A trip to the dentist should rule out or address a medical problem, and a consultation with an occupational therapist (O.T.) can give you methods to meet her oral sensory needs. When those needs are met, the behavior should decrease.

There's one other factor in changing the behavior—the environment. If you don't rid the environment of stressors, such as loud noises, arguing adults, or whatever else may send the child's sensory system into a panic, the behavior may still continue, simply because it's something predictable that she can control. Being surrounded by a peaceful, positive, supportive environment can be the greatest motivation for a person to strive to leave her world of repetition and isolation, to try to join those around her. This has been such an important factor in helping Lauren to join us that I've dedicated five other chapters to it!

Self-stim and challenging behaviors may not be huge problems for other families dealing with autism, but you've probably guessed that they have been significant aspects of Lauren's autism. I share the knowledge and the theories I've accumulated over the years in hopes that I'm mostly right and that something here is of help to you. However, I may be all wrong. Every birthday and Christmas, when Bryn and Craig ask, "What would you like?" I answer, "A day in Lauren's brain, so I can know what she's going through and I can really be of help." I haven't received this gift yet, but I'd settle for another. Even if she tells me I had it entirely wrong, I'd settle for sitting down and having a conversation with Lauren.

Positive Environment

I had no idea how I was going to say this in a book without it sounding negative, but here goes: When there's autism in the family, it encompasses absolutely every aspect of your lives. To test this theory, I asked my family members to say the first word or topic that came to them. I wanted to see if whatever they said, autism would have some bearing on it in our family. Bryn said, "Art." OK, Art:

- I've lost two paintings, a few ceramic pieces, and a variety of other items that might be considered art to "unforeseen autism-related" circumstancs.

- I can remember the day we had to put all art supplies in locked closets because Lauren became enamored of dumping (crayons were a favorite) and "skating"—using pieces of paper as skates on the hardwood floor.

- My hardwood floor is spotted turquoise in one room as the result of a memorable "tie-dye incident."

- We work at fine motor skills every day by modeling and encouraging Lauren to hold a crayon or marker or paintbrush, while encouraging her to look at what she is doing. She'll often hold the drawing instrument lately, but it's a well-celebrated event when she also watches her hand and appreciates what she's created.

Craig gave me a more difficult topic—"Birds."

- As soon as she was tall enough, Lauren opened up the birdhouse we had attached to the side of a tree and the nest inside fell to the ground. (Thank you, Lord, that the babies had already flown off by then.) At our house, we've learned that a birdhouse can be placed a few inches higher than the ideal height instructed on the label.

- When there are bird droppings on the swing set, Lauren will usually not avoid them, to her sister's dismay.

- When there's a hawk gliding and swooping on the side of the free-way, there are only three of us watching in awe.[26]

I've played this random naming game with myself in the past to try to discern if I'm crazy, or if there really isn't one area of my life that is not the least bit affected by autism. I've realized each time that I'm not crazy, but that, in fact, this is a disorder that challenges our family in every possible big and small way. Somehow, acknowledging this head-on is a relief every time. I can stop comparing my life with other fami-lies. I can stop wondering about when it might end and what "nor-malcy" might feel like. I can put all my thoughts and effort back into creating a positive environment where my unique and challenged fam-ily has the most opportunity for joy and success.

This chapter is actually about that positive environment my hus-band and I work so hard to create. A positive environment sounds like a pretty simplistic idea. It should be something everyone is striving to create in every situation of their lives. However, I rarely see that. I see people primarily using negative means, such as punishment and rejec-tion, to bring about a desired end. Though positive methods sound nice, negative methods seem more effective short term, and are more natural to human nature. When a child is misbehaving, for example, it's human nature for an adult to react negatively with ridicule or pun-ishment. This reaction gives the child nothing to help him behave the next time he's in a similar situation. You will likely have to up the ante each new incident. If Craig and I reacted negatively every time Lau-ren's actions were less than desirable, we would have run out of punishment for her years ago and then felt at a loss as to how to raise this child.

Thanks to some wonderful therapists, as well as lots of reading and listening, we have many positive methods up our sleeves. Over the years, these methods have become more than just a way to deal with behavior. The positive environment we've created has proven to be the strongest means of teaching Lauren new skills and keeping her in our world. To Craig and me, this isn't just a preferable form of discipline. It's a plan to be implemented. We simply can't afford to slip out of it as most people do a New Year's resolution.

Autism is an all-encompassing disorder and has the potential for destroying families. Creating a positive environment has been a means of saving our family. To us, being positive is equivalent to living our Christianity. It may also sound a lot like mere common sense with a little bit of the golden rule thrown in.

Craig and I look back at our personal histories and see how we were shaped and made ready (as ready as can be) for this vocation we were meant to share as husband and wife. Just today, I asked Craig, "Does the time we spent dating and falling in love seem like a distant memory that maybe didn't even happen? To me, it seems like that time was a surreal formality necessary to get to the marriage and the real stuff." Craig looked at me and nodded ever so slowly as though he had just had the same thought yesterday. (I can never shock this man with a bizarre thought anymore!)

What I'm trying to convey is this: Craig and I didn't one day rise out of despair because of some great discovery. We were already positive people working on creating a positive environment in our home before autism ever entered the picture.

My definition of a positive environment is one where unexpected moments of love and joy naturally occur, and occur pretty frequently—at least frequently enough to make up for the very difficult moments. A positive environment is a place a child (or any person) *wants* to be. A positive environment is also the best atmosphere for successful discipline.

I can remember, as a teenager, having a conversation with my mother about what hell was like. (For my family, such topics were common dinner-table "small" talk.) After a few suppositions were presented, I recall my mother saying, "I imagine hell to be knowing that you are dead forever and will never, ever see Heaven or the face of God. Can you imagine the anguish of that?" This is a good example, albeit a grand one, of how a positive environment can be quite motivational.

"Time-out" is popular among parents as a form of discipline, and it can be beneficial. If the environment from which the child is removed is one she enjoys, she will probably use that time away to do what's required to regain access. However, if the environment itself is the source of anguish that led to the misbehavior, the time away may be seen as a reprieve. For some children with autism, time-out is counterproductive as the child seeks to be alone, away from the stress that hinders her self-control. In this case, time-out is a reward for the child's behavior.

I'm reminded of this in my dealings with Lauren and her shoes. Lauren typically does not like to wear shoes. She puts them on, with our help, to go to the car and to go outside to play. She takes them off as soon as she gets into the car. Every now and then, she will also take them off outside while she's playing. Because we have so little grass and the dirt is frequently wet in our yard, I don't approve. One afternoon, after a few rounds of putting Lauren's shoes on again and again, I announced a consequence, "Take your shoes off again and you'll go inside." Lauren lasted a little while with her shoes on, but after a while, the shoes came off again, so I made her go inside. This became the normal routine outside. The shoes came off, the threat of inside was announced and the next time they came off, we went inside.

Eventually, Lauren needed a new pair of shoes. Though we hadn't been in the yard in a long while because of cold and wet weather, the new pair came off much less frequently in stores and in therapy. When we were finally headed out to the yard to play, I was thrilled to think that Lauren would keep her shoes on, and she did for awhile. But then they came off again, and we went inside. One day, Craig went outside with the girls and after a little while, I joined him. As I walked up to him, the frustration on his face and Lauren's shoes in his hands helped me to see the situation in a new light.

"Why did she suddenly take off her shoes?" he asked.

"That's how I trained her to tell me she wants to go inside," I answered. Craig looked at me and we both laughed. Since that day, I've begun asking Lauren earlier in our outdoor play sessions if she's ready to go inside. She regularly accepts the invitation before the shoes come off. Lately, Lauren will also, occasionally, just open the back door and walk into the house all by herself when she's ready to come in. I'm not sure whether it was motor planning difficulties that prevented her from making the transition on her own before, or something else, but I'll always have this reminder (and probably many more if I stop to think about it) of my ability to inadvertently motivate my child to "misbehave."

This story is one illustration of all the things that are needed to create a positive environment: empathy, respect, empowerment, and laughter. I must admit that I have never before categorized the qualities that make up a positive environment and the list looks simple and sparse. However, in the next four chapters, I'll share my thoughts on what makes up each of these categories, and the words simple and sparse will most likely not occur to you again.

Respect

Have you ever spent time with someone as an adult whom you were friends with as a child? Even if you're president of a bank or the highest paid speaker in the world, this person may still treat you like the kid who couldn't throw or catch a ball for anything. He may constantly remind you that you failed third grade, perhaps to reintroduce a more familiar pecking order. No matter what new information is presented during your time together, this old friend may turn out to be simply uninterested in the person you are today. Such a lack of respect probably would encourage you to avoid this person in the future.

Now imagine that you're a child with autism in a new classroom on the first day of school. All that the teachers know of you is from parental report and test scores. When it's time for the children to write their names on the board, a teacher says, "Oh, she can't write her name, so let's just have her press the button with her picture on it." When it's time for the morning announcements, the intercom buzzes and the new sound sends you into a fearful frenzy. "Now be quiet, the announcements are coming," says a teacher, then turns to the assistant and says, "She's known for throwing tantrums for no apparent reason and I'm just not going to put up with it in my class." In this classroom, there's no respect for the person you are today. Instead, you're the sum of reports and test scores. When you're non-verbal, that perception may be very difficult to change in a negative environment.

Showing respect for a person is not just a matter of manners and civility. It's a framework for addressing that person and making assumptions about that person. If you assume, without definitive proof, that a person possesses limited intelligence or capability, you are actually the one casting her in the role. You're no better than a coach at try-outs who sees a little guy and says, "You can be our water boy," rather than giving him the chance to prove he can throw, run and catch. Parents do this all the time. When a mom finds cookie crumbs on the counter and yells at a child, "I told you no cookies until after dinner!" she's assuming disobedience in her child with absolutely no proof. (It's whether she apologizes when her husband walks in with a cookie in his hand that determines if she's a lost cause.)

In the chapter about self-stimulatory behaviors, I mentioned some assumptions we should make when addressing children with autism.

First: There's an intelligent brain inside this person.
Second: This intelligent person wants the same basic things that every typical person wants: to be pain free, to be like others, to receive love, to feel good, to be as independent as possible, to be accepted, and to have something interesting to think about.

In other words, we assume a person is intelligent, that she's motivated by the same things that motivate us, and that she has good intentions, until there's proof to the contrary. It's the basis of the United States legal system: innocent until proven guilty. It's a simple matter of respect. It's also a guarantee that a person who can't easily express her needs won't have her voice silenced before it's ever found.

One evening, while our family was staying with relatives, the lady of the house was preparing dinner when I heard her say to Lauren, "No, no!" I walked into the kitchen as Lauren ran out and I asked, "What was she doing?" "She had the refrigerator door open," was the response. When people address Lauren in a situation, I often think about how they would address a speaking child in the same situation. For example, if Bryn were holding the fridge door open, would anyone come along and say, "No, no"? They would probably assume that she was looking for something to eat and would ask her what she wanted or tell her, "Dinner is almost ready, so let's not snack right now."

I asked how much longer dinner would be, then called Lauren back into the kitchen. I opened the refrigerator and pulled two snack options forward for her to see clearly. "Would you like pickles or grapes?" I asked. Lauren pointed to the pickles, walked over to the table, pulled a chair out and sat down to patiently await a plate of sliced pickles. When I assumed Lauren's behavior was prompted by needs and motivations customary of any eight-year-old, a communicative interaction was gained, she felt respected and her hunger was abated. When her behavior was dismissed as symptomatic of her autism, she was scolded, in effect, for having no voice.

Certain people in our lives ask us from time to time about Lauren's IQ and what "measurable" success she's shown. I think we could list one hundred successes Lauren's had in the last month, and their next question would be, "So, is she testing better than she was?" It's very important for some people to place a number on our child to determine…I'm not sure what they're trying to determine. Her value? What we should be doing with her? How they will address her? Many professionals also place a significant value on IQ scores. As I have said before, I have never seen any use made of an IQ score except to further limit a child's access to opportunity.

A few years ago, I listened to a renowned pediatric neurologist at an autism conference talk for most of his allotted time about how to perform different types of tests to assess the IQ of a child with autism. After his lecture, I stopped him and asked, "How can you get an accurate IQ on a person whose language you don't understand? Isn't it actually a measure of the degree of OUR misunderstanding of this person?" He said, "Oh, there are ways. True professionals have training so they can account for a person's difficulties." So, I asked, "What do you do to account for a child who completely shuts down when presented with a stressful situation, such as a testing situation?" He again assured me that professionals would know how to address such issues. I couldn't let him go so easily, so my last question was, "What are your thoughts on how much a person's IQ score should limit the opportunity offered him or her?" He looked at me like I had three heads and became distracted by another person, who, I listened long enough to ascertain, happened to be an admirer.

How could a purported expert on IQ not have thoughts on how the scores should be used? I believe he hasn't thought deeply on the issue, because he accepts the assumption that a person who appears of little brain *is* of little brain. Only his assumption is more educated: A person who *tests* of little brain is of little brain. (I wonder if he's ever thought about the fact that before IQ tests existed, phrenologists[27] were considered the experts on who was of little brain.)

I know a mom whose daughter has a lengthy diagnosis with autism referenced in there somewhere. This girl had been successfully communicating in private therapy with a communication device and it was time to extend this skill to the classroom, so a request for funding by the schools was made by the speech therapist, mom, and whomever else was necessary. Of course, this device was expensive, so teachers went to administrators and the matter was to be considered using proper channels. One day, an administrator called the mother and said her daughter had been re-tested. (She was not due for such testing for another six months.) The new tests showed her IQ to be lower than previously tested, and at this IQ level, such communication devices are not warranted. When the mother said she wanted to question this IQ score and this decision, she was told that, in fact, at this new IQ level, her daughter really didn't qualify to be in the class she currently attended (in which her daughter was very happy), so she might want to reconsider before drawing attention to this IQ score.

I was furious upon hearing this. Obvious questions popped into my head, like, "If she's been in this school for a length of time, wouldn't they feel responsible for a decreased test score? How does an IQ go down? Did someone bop her on the head and damage her brain even further? What does an IQ score have to do with this when the child has exhibited ability?" I lost contact with this mom after this conversation, but she's a bright enough lady that I'm sure the matter didn't end there. This wasn't the first time I'd heard of IQ scores being purposefully used to limit opportunity, which, in some cases, is done to save money.

I have lost count over the years of the number of parents I've met in books, articles and in waiting rooms who had professionals advise them to put their babies into institutional care because they foresaw a grim future of severe retardation, no hope for improvement and no redeeming value. The advice always goes something like, "Go on and live your life. This child will never walk" or "never talk." Of course, I wouldn't hear these stories if the child weren't exceeding all expectations—walking with braces at four years old, saying her first complete sentence at eight years old, or performing on stage at twelve years old.

Autism is a disorder for which there is no test, and is a label which is applied based on observable behaviors only. To ascertain mental retardation using those same behaviors (lack of speech, lack of eye contact) is quite circular. It reminds me of the question/answer game I've played with doctors in the past. It always goes something like this:

Q: "What is autism?" A: "A cluster of behaviors/symptoms."
Q: "What causes these behaviors?" A: "Autism"

For a test to be applicable, the person being tested must be able to respond in the format in which the test was written, or the difficulties surrounding the response must be fully understood and accounted for. This may happen in two ways: the person with autism communicates well enough to fully express her difficulties, so that the test may be adjusted accordingly; or new research shows exactly what's happening in the brain to cause the difficulties, so that they may be accounted for. This research is not yet available.

If I tell Lauren to put on her shirt and she fails to do so, that doesn't indicate that she's unable to dress herself. It doesn't indicate that she's unable to understand one-step directions. It doesn't indicate that her arms have range-of-motion difficulties. (It may signify that she prefers to be naked, thank you very much.) The only thing it definitely proves is that she reacts to this particular instruction in a fashion uncharacteristic of normally developing children. It is another sign of autism, though it doesn't show she has autism. It certainly doesn't signify that she's mentally retarded; particularly not when I can say, "Put on your shirt Lauren, then we'll have ice cream," and her shirt is over her head in a flash. (But that ice cream question probably isn't on the test, so she's out of luck.)

Autism is a disorder marked by inappropriate responses resulting from inaccurate perceptions. Until the reasons for these inaccurate perceptions are understood and accounted for (either by the autistic person being able to explain where the difficulties lie or research increasing our understanding) no test is valid. To say it is, and to use such a test to diagnose mental retardation or assign a low IQ score is completely disrespectful of the individual, as well as foolish. It's the same thing as going to a grocery store at 1:00 A.M., discovering that it's closed and the doors are locked, and proclaiming, "They must not have any apples in there."

I know my child can stack, suck through a straw and bring me an item upon verbal request. I've seen her do each of these things time and time again. She interacts with the world and with people all the time. However, in a testing situation, she will do nothing upon command, nor with a physical prompt. In fact, whenever someone is "waiting for her to perform," she may rock (though she rarely rocks in any other circumstance), squint her eyes and wiggle her fingers in front of her eyes. This is my daughter at her lowest level of ability to interact with her environment. This is also my daughter in a traditional testing situation.

The most respectful testing situation I have sat through with Lauren was in my home, which took away the first stressful factor affecting outcome—an unfamiliar environment. The psychologist asked me whether Lauren could perform certain tasks. She wrote down two scores next to each question. One was a measure of Lauren's performance during the testing situation. The other was her known ability according to parental report. The psychologist told me it was obvious that my daughter was very intelligent by the extent and type of eye contact she made, as well as her level of interaction with her mother. Though this psychologist wrote down scores for Lauren that were inaccurate, such as "three months" or "nine months" for developmental age levels, she qualified those numbers throughout her report, stating that Lauren's cognitive levels are much higher than she tested.

I'm not suggesting we shouldn't gauge where our children stand developmentally. It's valuable to know in what areas they are most behind so we can concentrate on these and measure improvement. However, having developmental age levels of "three months," "nine months" or even "twelve months" listed throughout a report on a child who is eight or ten years old serves only to alarm parents; it doesn't at all convey a child's strengths or where to start working with her. It's also simply bizarre to have "three months" listed anywhere as a developmental level when this child recognizes grandparents she sees once a year, remembers details of places she hasn't visited in two years, and can request videos and food using photographs.

The educational program we are currently using with Lauren has developmental levels numbered 1 through 6 under different developmental categories. Once levels are established, the goal is to move from one level to the next. The criteria for the next level are laid out for the parent, so goals are obvious. The organization provides a detailed individualized plan of action to help the child progress through the levels. This system is different from anything I have experienced before because the organization's theories on development differ from the mainstream. Though the lowest level in each category is a 1, and parents know exactly what level their child is in, the number isn't as frightening and unbelievable as a "mental age" like "three months." Though there are many benefits and reasons to the system, just this one is remarkable.

One day, one of Lauren's therapists, whom I'll call Angel, (because she is one) was a little upset about a situation she shared with me.

Because most of her clients see many other therapists and teachers, Angel often works with those professionals to ensure consistency among treatment plans, and to help the child's successes cross into other areas of life. Angel told me about a meeting she had been asked to attend by a client's psychologist. This young boy hadn't been performing certain tasks that were requested of him by the psychologist. Angel attended a session with plans to observe and hopes to offer suggestions. While Angel was observing, the boy performed every task that was requested of him. Angel was thrilled with his accomplishment and assumed the other professionals in the room were as pleased.

Afterward, the psychologist said to Angel in disgust, "He did that well only because you were here." (As though that was a bad thing and nothing was learned from the experience.)

After telling me the story, Angel said, "How about looking at it as 'Now we know he can do it, as well as what motivates him. How can we duplicate this success without me there? What's missing in this situation that this boy needs to be successful?'" Of course, what Angel provided to the educational setting is what she provides to this little boy, and all her clients—a positive environment and a loving relationship. If it's the loving relationship which motivates the child (and it usually is) then the psychologist now knows what he or she needs to work on to help this client be successful. Most normally developing children will work harder for people whom they respect and from whom they receive respect. I know that as a "normal" child I performed well for teachers I liked and performed horribly for those I disliked. As a "normal" adult, I strive to please those whom I respect and admire. How frustrating that some professionals expect children with disabilities to be motivated by different things than normally developing children. I don't know if developing a relationship with the child isn't specified in any textbook, or if some professionals are so focused on results they're afraid of investing time getting to know the child—time that may look unproductive on the books. Ironically, it's the relationship building that can bring the biggest pay-off in the long run.

I was sitting in the waiting room of a children's therapy center one day, when one of the regular clients arrived for her appointment. She's an adorable little girl who is tiny for her age and has a smile on her face every time I see her. She walked in slowly holding her mother's hand. When her physical therapist walked into the room, she said to the mom, "I'll take over from here," and put the little girl in a walker. (She never greeted the child.) It took that little girl at least fifteen minutes to slowly make her way down the hallway to the therapy room (as walking in the walker is part of her therapy, apparently). During that time, I couldn't help but notice that the therapist said nothing to the child except for an occasional, "C'mon."

I put myself in the girl's shoes and thought, "Why? I wouldn't want to go with you anywhere." At one end of the hallway is loving Mom in the waiting room, and at the other is this unexpressive, loveless therapist telling me to do things for no reason other than that we are scheduled to be together for an hour. I wouldn't have blamed the child if she had struggled to turn that walker around in the direction of the waiting room.

Of course, this therapist is not representative of the profession. There are other physical therapists in the same practice who obviously enjoy their work and their clients. Lauren has had a few therapists who have been warm and loving and have offered many suggestions and examples on how to create a positive environment for her. I've even shed tears at having to say goodbye to two of them. (She's also had a few who were mostly interested in how we would pay them each week, but each of those relationships was short-lived.) It astounds me when anyone in the field of disabilities is good at the paperwork, but bad at smiling and showing basic care and respect. If it's not about the people, why go into the field?

One day a few years ago, Bryn, Lauren and I were in our local Wal-Mart with a friend and we were ready to leave. There were two exits and as I headed toward the exit further from us, I simply explained, "Lauren needs to go out this door." My friend seemed frustrated, and I sensed that she thought I was being silly and that "door preference" had to be the most bizarre symptom of autism she had heard of yet.

When we were all settled into the car and on our way home, I revealed something very personal to my friend. "Sometimes, when I start my clothes dryer, I immediately have to go through my house and count my cats before I do anything else," I said. My friend looked at me like she was suddenly concerned that I was the one in the driver's seat. "Do you think that's weird," I asked her, "that I turn on my dryer then go and count my cats?"

"Well, why do you do it?" she had the presence of mind to ask before answering.

I told her this story. Not too long after we adopted Katie, one of our four cats, I was putting a load of dark clothes into the dryer and saw that Katie was making herself comfortable in there. (It took me a minute to notice her eyes among the clothes because she's entirely black.) I pulled her out, scolded her (for all that's worth), set her on the floor, then finished putting clothes into the dryer. My dryer was in the kitchen at the time, so I may have done a few things at the sink before finishing at the dryer, and I was also talking to Craig, who had walked into the room to tell me something during the process. I finally pushed the button to turn the dryer on and Craig and I stood there talking for a few minutes, when he suddenly laughed and said, "It sounds like there's a cat in the dryer."

I instantly heard what he was hearing. Along with the regular "rrrrrrrrrrr" sound of the dryer was a rhythmical noise that sounded like this: "mrah, (thud), mrah, (thud), mrah…" Craig tells me that as soon as he said that, my eyes grew huge and I said something like "Oh, no!" then ran to open the dryer door. My newest baby, my Katie, pulled herself up from the pile of steamy, warm clothes, and squinted her very dry eyes as I pulled her out while screaming, "My poor baby! I'm so sorry!" I was in tears and Craig was laughing hysterically. I was so worried that my kitten's legs were broken or that her eyes were cooked that my body was shaking. I hugged her for as long as she let me before she ran away to clean herself and pretend it never happened.

This incident left me so shaken that for a while, every time I turned on the dryer, I checked the whereabouts of my cats. When we adopted our third cat, Stella, who is also black, she jumped into the dryer with the clothes a few times. Even after pulling her out and making a visual check, I still had to verify the locations of all cats after pressing the start button. Right now, I'm not as frantic and I usually trust a visual check of the clothes when it's a light-colored load. But every now and then, I'll turn on the dryer at night and go to bed, only to get up a few minutes later, turn on the lights in every room of the house to find each cat in her sleeping nook before being able to lie down again and sleep.

"So, now do you think that's weird that I often count my cats after starting my dryer?" I asked my friend again. "No, that's pretty understandable after that," she said.

"Let me tell you another story," I said. And I told her about the time I was checking out at Wal-Mart and Craig decided to take Lauren to the car while waiting. Our Wal-Mart is across the street from the runway of a Naval Air Base and they are often doing maneuvers in the immediate area. The fighter jets and cargo planes that fly past are often deafening. (To better illustrate: I've been in a parking lot during maneuvers where the sound and vibration of the jets set off the alarms of every car in the parking lot.) That day, Lauren and Craig had taken a few steps out the automatic exit door, when a frighteningly loud jet suddenly screamed past overhead. Lauren immediately turned around and ran back into the store, gripping her dad's hand and dragging him with her. They met me back at the checkout, where Craig, respecting Lauren's fright, tried not to chuckle as he told me the story. When I was finished, we headed toward the door again, but as we neared it, Lauren stopped and began pulling us in the opposite direction. Despite our reassurances, there was no way she was going out that super loud door again! Thankfully, there was another exit, so we agreed to turn around and she happily walked out the "quiet door."

"To this day," I told my friend, "Lauren remembers what door in what store made that frighteningly loud noise when it opened and refuses to go through it. We're pretty impressed that she remembers it so well and we respect that she still has fear associated with it. So, just as Craig doesn't tell me I'm stupid, or laugh at me, or force me to lie down and not check the cats at night, we don't force her to go through a door that's given her such a fright."

"Oh, I see," said my friend. Then she talked to Lauren in the back seat about what a fright that must have been, with a respect I'd never heard in her voice, certainly not when speaking to Lauren.

Since that day in the car with my friend, Lauren has realized the nearer door in Wal-Mart doesn't always make that sound and she'll walk through it happily. I credit her understanding to the time I took advantage of a peaceful shopping trip, when I knew Lauren was in good form as we were leaving Wal-Mart. I told her, as we neared the door and it opened for someone else, "Oh, that door is quiet today. I think we can go through it." Then I "firmly" escorted her through. That's all it took for a thorough healing. Now, I wish someone could do that for my cat-in-the-dryer phobia.

So many people today operate according to the theory: "If I don't understand you, you're wrong or weird." Craig and I try to maintain a better approach: "If I don't understand you, I need to try looking from a new angle, preferably from the position you're standing in." I'd like to believe we've been this enlightened for a very long time, but it's more likely that Lauren has taught us the better approach. It seems that when you consistently show respect for someone, the next natural step is to develop empathy for that person.

Empathy

I should have known better. I had been cleaning the tops of my kitchen cabinets where I kept many tins and see-through storage containers. The tins held matches, keys, cookie cutters, etc. The glass containers held staples such as rice, beans, pasta and cornmeal. These containers were covered with dust and so were now scattered across my kitchen counters awaiting their turn in the sink. As is always the case with these stories, I have no idea what diverted my attention and took me away from the task. Most likely I had checked on Lauren, found a mess she'd created and shooed her away from the room as I cleaned it up. (Most disasters in our house come in threes, thanks to this predictable cycle.)

As I walked to the kitchen to get back to the original job, I stopped short in the doorway at the sight before me. My little four-year-old was sitting in the middle of the floor covered with cornmeal. The floor around her was covered with cornmeal. The counters were covered with cornmeal. And I fully appreciated in an instant, as mothers do, that there was cornmeal in the stovetop burners and in every unreachable nook and crevice in every appliance and in between cupboards and appliances. My ire instantly rose as the picture of how I would spend the next few hours solidified itself in my brain.

"Lauren Therese!" I screamed. Lauren looked up. I could see her pale green eyes flash open at me, then look down, a nervous head bob and body rock beginning. I also recalled, mercifully, that just that morning her occupational therapist told me how much Lauren had enjoyed playing in the rice bin. Here I had left a container of cornmeal (with no lid on it) at about the eye level of a little girl who was being encouraged to run her hands through a bucket of rice just four hours earlier.

"Well, I see you found the cornmeal," I changed my tone, and Lauren looked up at me again for an instant. I looked at the large container (which had once held much more cornmeal than we would ever use in one year) and I saw that there was about an inch left in the bottom. I tiptoed across the slippery floor and over Lauren, picked up the container, and poured the yellow sandy stuff over my fingers so that it rained down in front of her face. Lauren squinted at the yellow coming down, lifted her hand so she could feel it through her fingers too, and laughed. I scooped as much cornmeal off the counters as I could find to continue the game while Lauren played in what fell in her lap and in front of her. Then I took Lauren by the hands, pulled her to her feet and we danced. As we slid across that floor, I was supporting her, humming a song and leading in the messiest but most memorable dance I've ever had with my daughter, or anyone, to date. Lauren may have thought I'd gone nuts, but she stayed with me, smiling and chuckling, until it was finally time to face the reality of a bath and the broom.

This is just one incident which reminds me daily that I can't expect my child to be successful if I've set her up for failure. I know my daughter has extreme tactile sensory needs and she seeks to meet them with harsh sensations, such as sand and pinecones. She also seeks the visual stimulation of many small shapes moving past her eyes. At the time this happened, she hadn't yet reached a level of understanding that some things are off limits. The situation I had left in the kitchen was an invitation to disaster. I might as well have asked an alcoholic to pour me a glass of wine.

Another of Lauren's tactile needs which has required quite a bit of empathy from me is her desire to strip or to be naked. (There's a big difference. Sometimes I think it's the throwing off of the clothes that gives her satisfaction. Other times she just seems to enjoy the feel and freedom of nudity.) This has been one of the most challenging aspects of Lauren's autism. It made toilet-training messier and more difficult.

It also makes visiting (particularly with priests and friends with sons) frequently awkward. As she grows older and taller, even Lauren's favorite spot—standing in front of the living room picture window—is a difficulty. Besides being concerned about Lauren's dignity, I'm afraid some neighbors may eventually report the free peep show they're getting from the road.

Not long after Lauren was diagnosed, I heard a story about an autistic woman who tended to strip, very quickly and unexpectedly, in public. One day, after this woman stripped naked in a grocery store aisle, the person with her asked, "Why did you do that?!" I don't recall if the woman responded verbally or through an alternate communication system, but she expressed something to the effect of, "I just feel yucky in here and I had to get it off me." The woman later conveyed that the feeling she wanted to get off her was the stress she was undergoing in that situation at the moment. Years later, when Lauren started stripping, I remembered this lady and looked for patterns in Lauren's stripping. One reason Lauren strips is definitely to get attention. I'm sure the stripping came first, as she had to learn that she would get attention by doing it; but when she quickly strips in one room, then immediately streaks through another (more populated) room with a big grin on her face, the intent is obvious.

The second pattern, which took me longer to see, was Lauren's stripping off her clothes pretty quickly upon coming into the house after an outing. Lauren's stress during many outings is palpable, so the theory that she was reacting to her inward stress in an outward way like the lady in the previous story seemed very likely. However, I didn't recall any solution to the problem. (Empathy is great for lending understanding, but it's priceless when it also leads to a solution.) I came up with my own solution. If the stress she felt was linked to her clothing, Lauren's reason for stripping in these instances seemed quite appropriate, so I didn't want to teach her it was wrong. In fact, I was proud of her for keeping her clothes on the entire time she was in public. So, to this day, whenever we come home from an outing, we bring new clothes with us into the bathroom, attend to any toileting needs, then I help her completely change her outfit. I talk about her being all done with the place of the outing and changing into fresh clothes. Though she may still leave the bathroom and strip, she more often keeps her new outfit on.

I become frustrated when I hear people say things like, "Keep your clothes on." Or "No, we don't get naked." There is nothing inherently wrong with being naked. The wrong comes in when the issue of *where* people may be naked comes up. What must Lauren think when, within the same hour of hearing she shouldn't strip, someone tells her, "OK, let's take your clothes off and hop into the bath." I think she's now well aware of the many times and places where nudity is unacceptable and the very few times and places where it is acceptable. But when a child's comprehension level is unknown or she is in an early learning stage, confusion reigns when absolutes are used. There are so few times when the words *always* and *never* are applicable. Phrases specific to the situation, like "*Right now,* we need to keep our clothes on" or "We keep our clothes on *in the store*" ensure a rule won't appear useless soon after being taught.

In order to provide Lauren every opportunity to be successful, I need to address her many sensory needs—those of which I'm aware—then be as empathetic as possible to the needs I don't yet understand. There are many things that send Lauren into a state of panic or stress. Sometimes, despite our best efforts, she's allowed to stim long enough to work herself into a frenzy. This is often hard to address because we can't see what's going on inside of her until her outward reaction turns into a full-blown tantrum. Other times, the source of panic comes from outside of her. No matter how peaceful and healthy she's feeling on the inside, Lauren's guaranteed to go to pieces if she's forced into a *chaotic* or *negative* environment for any length of time. For those who don't understand what I mean by a chaotic environment, step inside a Chuck E Cheese restaurant sometime. (Though, if you've heard of them and think you can imagine it without a trip, spare yourself. I've never set foot in one. Craig's colorful description is enough for me.)

A negative environment is a little more difficult to predict, as it's less obvious and can sneak up on you. We don't take Lauren into stores that play a variety of music at the same time, or have an assortment of strong scents that greet you as you walk in, such as candle or bath supply stores. If something in a new environment challenges our own healthy nervous systems, we imagine that her unhealthy system will have a harder time coping. (She's proven this theory many times.)

Our own house can be a negative environment when disagreements or too many commitments are causing a lot of stress or tension between family members. No matter how much pretending we do, Lauren is gifted when it comes to being in tune with the truth. She can tolerate only so much of her parents being mentally preoccupied or agitated before the stress it creates in her boils over into behavior. Even strangers in public can create a negative environment by casting glares at Lauren for her misunderstood behavior. I'm not sure if Lauren picks up on the disdain of the reproaching people or the stress it induces in her parents; whatever the cause, she quickly becomes upset.

Many years ago, when Lauren was just a toddler or slightly older, a friend and I met at a local McDonald's for lunch with our children. This had become a weekly outing for my family because Lauren's therapy was scheduled around lunchtime and this particular McDonald's had a very nice playland with things other than the usual tube slides. (We've always avoided those tubes. I figure that if Lauren ever enters one, she'll never come out of her own free will, and I am *not* going in after her.) We almost always sat at the same table in the playland and the children always ate the same thing—chicken nuggets and french fries.

This particular day, we decided that my friend would get the food inside and I would take her daughter and my two out to the playland to situate them at the table. When I walked out the door, I saw that where we ordinarily sat was empty of people, but there were five little meals of chicken and french fries all laid out on wrappers around the table. "Oh, no!" I thought, as I approached the table and quickly surveyed the area for another empty table big enough for five. But a hungry Lauren had already seated herself at "her" table, ready to dig into her customary order, which was placed right in front of her where her mommy always put it. I was heartbroken for her, since I knew my explanation about this being someone else's food at someone else's table would make no sense to her. When she refused to budge and I began struggling to drag her away from the table, I grew angry. I knew no one had malevolent intent when they placed *Lauren's usual lunch* at *Lauren's usual table* with no bodies there to give my story about someone else's lunch a shred of proof. Yet, I still may have had a hint of anger in my voice as I attempted to shout above Lauren's screams in the direction of the play equipment, "Is this somebody's lunch sitting here unclaimed?!" Two moms quickly gathered three little boys from the play equipment and ushered them to their table. I never made eye contact with them, mostly because I was still dragging my screaming daughter (who can make herself as solid as a sack of potatoes and as unwieldy as an octopus all at the same time) across the ground to another table.

When I finally pulled Lauren up to a seat at the new table, she had stopped struggling, but was now sobbing, with an occasional scream and hitting of the table thrown in. She wasn't hurting anyone and had accepted that she couldn't go back to that other table, despite the fact that, yes, all indicators declared it hers. So I rubbed her back and repeated over and over to her in as peaceful a voice as I could muster, "Your chicken's coming, Lauren. You're doing such good waiting." While saying this, I caught the eye of an elderly man who was sitting nearby and staring at me in disgust. All I could think of to say to him was, "You're the one who chose to sit in the kids' playland!" and worse, so I kept my mouth shut.

When my friend finally arrived with the food, you can imagine her surprise and distress at what she found. After food was in front of everyone and Lauren was calm enough to chew in between pitiful little gasps of air, I told my friend the story. Then she said something that is one of many reasons this friend is so dear to me. She said ever so lovingly, "Lauren, I'm so proud of you. You did such good waiting."

When a negative environment is unavoidable, the best defense is a good offense. Children with sensory processing disorders, such as autism, can't learn to cope with sensory challenges while being hurt by them. They need to be supported and taught in a positive environment surrounded by loving people. In a positive environment, a child is respected, her ability to understand and relate to the world is always taken into consideration and her needs are honored. This encourages her to interact with the world without fear of unexpected reproach for doing only what she knows how to do.

For Lauren, and for most children with autism, an environment of peace and predictability is the best learning environment. It provides them the opportunity to explore their world without fear of the unexpected around every corner. That's not to say that these kids like things to remain stagnant and forever the same. In fact, once Lauren has shown me or a therapist that she can do something, she usually has no inclination to do it again. We believe she operates under the theory, "I've done that once for you. This isn't a recurring carnival act for your amusement. If you weren't quick enough to catch it the first time, that's your loss."

The type of predictability of which I speak is the same kind you would want if you were asked to make a speech to a large audience. (Many of the day-to-day demands we place on Lauren are as challenging to her as such a speaking engagement would be to me.) If travel is involved, you would want to know the airline's schedule and to have the plane be on time. You would want to know the layout of the room, whom you will follow on the dais, and what sort of people will be in attendance. All this information helps you to plan a proper speech (act appropriately) and reduce your stress. Things may still not go as planned (the location could change or the sound system could malfunction as you step up to the microphone), but your preparations give you an overall understanding of the situation. This understanding enables you to address individual problems as they arise, rather than lose all confidence and capability at the first complication.

We create order out of chaos for ourselves all the time. This is why people live out of their daily planners and Palm Pilots: so they'll avoid scheduling bumps in the road, but will have the tools available to address those bumps when they're unavoidable. Providing our children with similar tools on a daily basis will help them in the same way—by giving them the means to create order out of chaos when chaos is unavoidable. The McDonald's story illustrates a situation in which all the rules Lauren operated by at the time were broken. In an environment in which she was normally peaceful and successful, there were so many unexpected changes that she was left with no applicable rules with which to recreate order. If I had said, "Behave!" and she had understood me, her thoughts would have correctly looked something like this: "But I've been following every rule you've ever taught me about McDonald's and you're telling me I'm wrong!"

Using a schedule is just one way to help create order. Even when Lauren wouldn't look at a schedule, having it posted and announcing what was coming next helped *me* to stay on track and made me less likely to throw her a curve ball without warning. Even without a schedule, telling a person what's coming next (or showing pictures if that's more meaningful) helps her to prepare in whatever way is necessary for the next event. I keep photographs in my pocketbook of all the stores, restaurants and people we tend to visit, so that if we decide while on the road to go somewhere, I can help Lauren plan for this unexpected turn of events. If there's a choice we can allow her to make, we show her two or three photos. She points to one and is thrilled to have a say in the plans. (We're even more thrilled when she says the name of the place—a rare but precious occurrence.) If it's a new place we tell her it's new, as well as everything about it that we think may help her. We've even found that if we know nothing about the new place, expressing our excitement about it in an excited voice helps Lauren to prepare her body for the excitement (or stress) she may soon feel. Lauren always seems to appreciate whatever kind of heads-up we can offer.

When Lauren was a toddler, we realized that the sounds of vacuum cleaners and train whistles frightened her, so we began announcing the approach of both. "Vacuum cleaner, Lauren!" I still announce in a pitch and volume closer to that of the vacuum cleaner than my own, readying her ears for the next step up. "I see a train coming! Whoo whoo!" I call to the backseat upon hearing a rumble up the tracks parallel to the road. Of course, the sudden surprise of the loud noises is probably what most startled and upset her, as it does many people. For quite a while now, Lauren hasn't become upset when an unexpected train whistles past or when a vacuum cleaner is turned on unannounced. She's learned to read the signs as we all did as children: *When I hear Mom roll the heavy Electrolux across the floor, I know that loud nasty whir is coming next.* But I still make the announcement. Her sensitive body probably feels the rumble of a train in the distance long before I do, so when I call out that it's coming, I wonder if she's a little concerned about my delayed reaction.

Many children and adults, including myself, require a sense of order before they can move on to higher business. For Lauren, this higher business includes social interaction, communication and many other skills used daily by most people who don't give them a single thought. Helping someone to predict and plan is one means of creating order. Another way is to designate and maintain boundaries.

Some physical boundaries are obvious. When Lauren was younger, she needed to explore the entire periphery of each new environment before she could feel comfortable enough to explore the other things and people there. Once she decided on the circumference of a new place, she would continue to walk in circles, allowing the circles to shrink and change shape. After a while, she would include short stops to pick up objects and to touch and smile at people. One hazard related to Lauren's need to know her boundaries is that when she finds that a boundary has expanded (i.e. she finds an open door or window) she goes through it to continue her exploration until she once again comes to a barrier.

We've experienced losing Lauren out an open door two different times at friends' houses. Each time, there was a party in progress, and Craig and I both thought the other one was with Lauren at the moment. One time, we saw each other at the same time and asked, "Do you have Lauren?" Almost in the same instant, someone came walking through the front door announcing that some little girl just ran out. I thought afterward, "Why didn't you think to stop her? We're about twenty-five feet from a busy street!" But at that moment, Craig bolted out the front door and I bolted out the side. Craig reached Lauren first at the end of the sidewalk, grabbing her just as she was about to turn toward the street. The possibility of losing an exploring Lauren to an on-coming car or other tragedy often haunts me in dreams.

Though today Lauren is much better at turning around and coming back when she's called, we still actively practice staying within boundaries that are only visual, such as the edge of our front yard, which is marked by driveways. Lauren's desire to keep running across the driveway to explore new terrain is obvious, as she often just stands on the driveway's edge, inching closer and closer to it. Sometimes she gives in to temptation and actually runs across the driveway and into the neighbor's yard. The consequence of crossing that boundary is to lose the privilege of playing in the front yard. She has to go inside or into the fenced back yard. Lauren's need to explore must be pretty strong for her to risk losing the front yard adventure she apparently enjoys very much.

Boundaries aren't just unsurpassable physical barriers. Anything which provides a framework for understanding is a boundary. When we say "Eat at the table, Lauren" or "Sit to eat" then take her food away when she stands up to leave, we're creating boundaries surrounding eating. The table itself provides physical boundaries for her body while she eats, and visual boundaries for her food and place setting. When we are consistent with these boundaries, they provide a predictable framework in which Lauren can explore many new things in the world of food and in social interaction.

I remember the first time Lauren ever just "hung out" with anyone outside our home. I was sitting with a friend at her dining room table just enjoying after-dinner conversation. The food and dishes had been cleared, so Lauren's customary motivation wasn't present when she sat in the chair across from me and smiled from one of us to another. Every now and then she would mumble a sound or two, look back and forth between us, then chuckle. She was either mimicking us or doing a fine job of joining in the conversation, or perhaps a little of both. Lauren has never joined in this way for living room conversation. The rules and arrangement of people and furniture may be too complicated to give her a comfortable framework for understanding her part in this environment. When we have people over, we often have what we call "table parties." We spend most of our visiting time at the table because that is where Lauren is most likely to join us. I haven't heard any complaints about this arrangement, probably because all family members and most friends are big fans of dessert.

Some people say that children who work best within firm boundaries will have a hard time in the real world because they won't be able to generalize their knowledge to other social situations. Most of these people haven't met my daughter, because her home and family *are* her real world. There's not a great chance she'll be asked out to a dance and have that table-socializing thing stand in the way of her success. (If she does get asked, that means we've come a long way fast, so she probably would be able to learn "ballroom etiquette" quicker than we could find a dress.) It's when children have a firm grasp of foundational information, and have had opportunities to be successful and to feel successful that they are ready to tackle more worldly assignments.

A common occurrence in many households is for families to eat popcorn while watching a movie. In our family, that didn't happen for years. We had been so consistent with the boundary, "Keep food at the table, Lauren," that she ripped snacks out of our hands and took them to the dining room table when we dared to sit on the sofa or recliner with them. When my daughters were young, I remember explaining to visitors that there could be no eating in the family room because it upset Lauren. One guest's response wasn't a happy one. She suggested that Lauren's problem with snacks in the family room had something to do with a lack of discipline instead of a lack of understanding. But my guests obliged my request.

Recently, I made some popcorn while we were watching a kids' movie we had rented. At first, Lauren became very upset. She took her popcorn to the dining room, sat down, and whined and cried over the insubordination in the living room. I decided to try something. Our small kitchen table was in the living room at the time, as the base for a four-foot Christmas tree during the holidays. I carefully took the tree and skirt off the table and set them in the corner of the room. Then I pulled a kitchen-table chair up to the table and went to get Lauren's popcorn and drink. "Look, Lauren," I said as I brought her popcorn bowl to the living room table and set it down. "Eat your popcorn at this table." Lauren slipped into the chair and began eating her popcorn once again, keeping her eyes on the movie all the while. The table and chair were behind the upholstered furniture in the room, so one of us would look back at her from time to time and ask, "Hey, how are you doing in the balcony, Sweetie?"

It was a memorable moment for us all, sharing popcorn in front of a movie, as well as Lauren's company. I thought about the slow but steady transition process that had finally brought us to this day. Within about five years, Lauren went from not tolerating utensils or dishes of any kind to eating out of bowls and off plates with a spoon or fork. She went from spending meal times screaming in her bedroom (because she had hit us and pushed us out of our chairs at the table) to being interactive at meals and enjoying them thoroughly. She also went from hiding out when people visited to sitting at the table with company for the sole purpose of being together. I think I'm glad I didn't just say "Too bad for you, Lauren" all those years ago instead of denying my guests popcorn in the comfortable chairs. I'll bet they've had plenty of opportunities to eat popcorn in front of their TV over the years. And this past month, our whole family did, too.

Empowerment

Helping a person to predict and plan is one way to create order out of potential chaos. Providing boundaries is another way. A story I told previously about Lauren circling our backyard (then coming out of her shell to include us in her circle) is one example of a predictable boundary providing an atmosphere for success. Another example is an event I'll always vividly remember in which another naturally-occurring boundary provided an atmosphere of success.

One June day, we were still housing three of six rescued kittens in a large cage in our carport. These kittens had no mama with them when Craig and three-and-a-half year old Lauren found them in a dirty and dilapidated box in the park at the end of our street. (To make a long story short, Craig came home to tell me about them, I sent him back with food and water, and they *followed* him back down the street, trotting six in a row behind him like he was mama. Three were pretty quickly adopted, so we were down to three this particular afternoon.)

Where we live, tornadoes are the climatic calamity of choice, so every resident is well aware of where they will run to when the tornado siren sounds. Because we have no basement, we were still experimenting with potential tornado hideouts this particular day. Craig was looking out the window and following radio reports of sightings while I readied our bedroom closet as shelter. I removed all the shoes and clothes from lower racks, while the girls played with flashlights on my bed. When a huge wind picked up and I realized the rain was blowing horizontally at the windows, I checked on the kittens in the carport and they were drenched! I brought them inside, just as Craig suddenly announced, "OK, it's time to get in there!"

I took Lauren by the hand to join an excited Bryn. I worried the confinement might frighten Lauren, who at the time was often in her own little world, except for the occasional tantrum when the unexpected occurred. (At this time, she found looking at people's faces difficult and never gave hugs, only accepting them on occasion. Her words were few and far between.) We closed the door and lit our flashlights. To our surprise, Lauren was more pleased with this situation than we had ever seen her. I recounted this event in her journal, in which I addressed Lauren directly:

*During the tornado that brought the three kittens inside, you discovered that your family was really cool. When Mommy and Daddy gathered Bryn, you and the kittens and brought them into our dinky bedroom closet, we thought you would completely freak out. But you loved it! I had a flashlight and you sat on my lap facing me and checking out my face. You had a big smile on your face and seemed to be checking to see if I was smiling (i.e. playing a big, funny joke!) Lauren, Mommy hugged you and **you hugged me**, over and over again, simply seeming so pleased that your family had given in to the ways of the closet people—those who saw value in reducing external stimuli and shutting "the world out." You seemed pleased as punch that we'd finally entered your realm—we'd seen the light while sitting in the dark! When I said, "I love you" to you, you repeated it to me so meaningfully, **"I love you."***

When Daddy finally decided the worst was past us, Bryn and he left with the kittens, but Lauren and Mommy stayed awhile in the closet. When I finally did get up and leave, you came and got me, and Daddy and Bryn, and brought us all back inside the closet and closed the door. You didn't want it to end, Baby!

Despite the fact that I had played no intentional part in bringing it about, this is a great example of a positive environment empowering a person. In an environment which addressed all her physical needs, she was capable of looking into people's faces with expression and expectation, and of saying a three-word sentence, "I love you." I can count on one hand the number of times we have heard Lauren utter those words again, and certainly never as clearly as that day in that beautiful, impromptu situation.

Over the years, we've tried to reproduce the situation which occurred on that stormy day in the closet, but Lauren's reaction has never been as remarkable. There must have been factors involved in her success over which we had no control. However, our family has discovered many factors over which we do have control.

Sound has been one environmental factor that has obviously been a consistent influence upon Lauren's abilities. When she was very young, Lauren was frightened of many sounds, particularly high pitched and unexpected ones. We began playing a variety of peaceful classical music at home, and Lauren's tolerance of such noises quickly increased. Though we have never participated in any formal sound therapy for Lauren, the benefits of playing great works at home was obvious. I recommend it to everyone. It's easy, inexpensive and may greatly contribute to the parents' and siblings' state of mind and ability to cope, as well.

After a long while of playing only classical pieces for Lauren, my husband started introducing her to some of his favorites whenever I wasn't home. I would be greeted at the door with, "She loves Eric Clapton, but can only take so much Stevie Ray Vaughn." We started playing a variety of radio stations while in the car and came to the conclusion that Lauren's consistent favorite is country music. (More along the lines of Garth Brooks than more traditional "cryin', lovin' and leavin'" country.) Lauren's preferences are always clear and consistent. Once in awhile, though, she won't be in the mood for a typical favorite and it's refreshing to have her communicate that she wants the music changed. It reassures us that she does care, and that, more often than not, we do meet her musical needs.

Music isn't useful just as a background, calming influence. Sometimes, it's my primary means of helping Lauren to calm down and to be able to rejoin us. Particularly when Lauren was a baby and toddler, I recall her waking up in the middle of the night seeming terrified. No matter what reassurance we offered, she didn't seem to recognize us. She cried and screamed, even while trying to nurse. Like any mom, I often sat with her in the rocking chair and rocked her for comfort. On nights when she was this far gone, I rocked with a fury. I had to pull Lauren back out to reality, but my voice and my touch weren't reaching her, so I used rhythm. I rubbed her body firmly in time with the rocking. I sang familiar songs and rocked and rubbed in rhythm to the music. And always, Lauren would eventually come out of whatever horrible place she was in and relax.

Music has been invaluable in keeping Lauren focused, calm and with us. When stress is encroaching due to her messed-up sensory system, music often helps change her mood by changing her focus. I think of Lauren's becoming behaviorally difficult and inaccessible as being like a person losing his glasses and hearing aid all at once. Lauren seems not even to hear or see what we're doing to try to help her, she's so caught up in the anguish going on inside of her. In order to readjust her focus from the inside (what's troubled) to the outside, I need a passive tool—something that doesn't require her cooperation, just her presence, like a pair of glasses. A strong rhythm is inescapable to a body's autonomic system and will elicit some kind of response without a person's even being aware. It's this inevitability that I count on. When Lauren does gain the presence of mind to acknowledge the music in some visible way, such as by smiling, calmly moving in time, or by approximating some lyrics, I'm sure I've won her back.

Lauren doesn't often become as frantic and inaccessible as she did when she was younger. When she does, there is an obvious, physical reason for it, such as a visit to the doctor, dentist, or hairdresser. (We've sung Lauren through many annual checkups and haircuts. I'm sure our loving hairdresser, Kirsten, is quite enthralled with Craig's and my rendition of "'A' You're Adorable".) When the cause isn't quite as obvious, we look for a physical reason and I don't recall ever being disappointed. Every time I feel ready to throw in the towel during a lengthy bout of difficult behavior, we learn that Lauren has an ear infection, strep throat or some other understandable reason to be upset.

No matter what the circumstance, music is one means of empowering Lauren with the greatest opportunity to be successful. Daily exposure increases her ability to cope and join us on a regular basis. More directed music targets the most challenging moments, often serving as a lifeline when things look most bleak for us all.

Many people acknowledge that autism affects a person's ability to focus, but the extent to which focus is affected is generally unknown if the person has trouble communicating such information. Just as we use music to draw Lauren's focus in a positive direction, we do everything we can to strengthen her ability to maintain focus, as well as to compensate for her lack of focus. The most obvious way to do this is to bring what we wish her to focus on to the front and center. Ironically, for people with autism who have stronger peripheral vision than central vision, bringing something "front and center" visually may mean pushing it further away or off to the side. I see this most in Lauren at the table. When she was younger, she often became focused on the plates of people across the table from her or next to her and would become angry. I would tell her, "You have the same food they have," but I needed to push her plate further away from her so that it would catch her attention. Then she could readjust her focus and see that she did have the same food in front of her.

Any type of teaching which requires Lauren to focus on something visual, such as a book or paper to draw on, has often proven more successful when I move the object around until it catches her eye. We start from there, rather than wasting time trying to coax her to look down in front of her, where the book or paper would be in a traditional setting.

As you continue to work with a child, presenting meaningful information in a useful way, her ability to focus centrally becomes stronger. Currently, I can ask Lauren to look at what I am holding in front of her and she will consistently look. Her auditory focus has also improved over the years. Considering that she didn't respond to any sound at the time she was diagnosed, it has improved drastically. I believe that our conscious effort to adjust our speech so that meaning is as accessible as possible has been an important factor in her success. Though I'm sure I did this early on (as a mom who read books on parenting and tried to maintain a loving environment) I didn't recognize how important it was until I attended my first autism conference.

In a workshop offered by Carole Swick[28] on behavioral management, I asked how she would recommend handling a predictable scenario at our house: Lauren goes to the door and communicates that she wants to go outside, but we can't go outside at the moment and I tell her so. Lauren acts like I just didn't understand the request and continues to gesture, using every means to indicate that she wants to go outside, until she is upset, throwing a tantrum, then exhausted. Though I don't remember Carol's exact wording, she explained that when my child hears a "No," that's all she probably hears. Though I may say, "No, we're not going outside right now. Let's eat lunch," she probably didn't hear anything past that very upsetting "No."

"Tell her what will happen rather than what won't happen," said Carol. "Tell her, 'We're staying inside right now.'" Using positive terms creates a mental picture of what is to come. This is more helpful to the child than just trying to eliminate the existing picture in her head, but providing nothing to replace it.

My practice at using positive terms greatly benefited me during the year I taught a Sunday School class of one-year-olds. Week after week, parents would comment on how well I managed this large group of children. When I walked into this job, snack time went from a free-for-all throughout the morning to a mid-session event that occurred at the table only. (I set boundaries.) People were amazed that I could get ten to fifteen one-year-olds to sit at a table for their entire snack time. My "secret" was simply knowing that a one-year-old's ability to focus on the spoken word is limited.

When you consistently inform that "We sit to eat" and "Food stays on table," children quickly develop a clear picture of what they are *sup-*

posed to do. When a child whines and points at the snack cupboard fifteen minutes before snack-time, happily informing him that, "Yes, snack is coming next!" can make him very happy. Imagine, if in each of these circumstances, I responded, "No, don't get crumbs on the floor," or "No, no cookies right now." I might as well say, "Please cry right now, little boy," since I'm accomplishing the same thing. I'm asking a child with limited understanding to take what he does understand and wipe it out of his mind. In offering positive words, I'm empowering the child by handing him a new picture, a new understanding of the situation.

Carole Swick also spoke about using variables on a regular basis to help a child understand when things are different from what's desired or expected. For example, say "*Sometimes* we go to Wendy's and *sometimes* we go to McDonald's" or "*Today*, we're going to Grandma's house. *Tomorrow*, we'll go see Vicki." My favorites are "first" and "then." "*First* we eat lunch, *then* we go outside." I can see Lauren's brain working in her reaction to these words. She is obviously trying to stay calm with the reassurance that what she wants is coming, she just has to wait out what I said must come first. It provides her with a lot more useful information and hope than a simple "No, not now" offers.

Using variables helps a child to predict and plan, even for eventualities. I know from experience that when we drive down certain roads, Lauren expects that we're headed for a familiar destination. For example, Lauren loves to swim. One day, we were riding in the car down the road we most often took for the purpose of going to our community pool. This time, instead of turning right at the stop sign, as I would to go to the pool, I went straight. Lauren instantly became frantic. I realized that my going straight did not jibe with her understanding of the situation. Also, like any child, she was very disappointed and had no idea what to do with this disappointment. This reaction has occurred many times while we were driving on familiar roads, but to a new destination. As I gain wisdom, however, I remember to talk to Lauren about our destination (planting a positive picture of what's to come) before her incorrect expectations become rooted.

Our family uses positive terms all day long to help Lauren bear the otherwise unbearable, to help her to focus, and to help her stay calm. For Lauren, getting a haircut, her nails trimmed or her teeth brushed are all aversive experiences, thanks to her challenged sensory system. But after years of our using positive strategies to help her, she regularly sits still for all three events with varying degrees of physical support. When it's time to trim her nails and she's having a hard time allowing me to hold onto her fingers, I reassure her with a goal, such as, "Finish this hand, then we'll take a break." In the early days, nail trimming could be a one-finger-at-a-time, two-day experience. Currently, when I bring the clippers over and say, "Time to trim our nails," Lauren typically holds her hand up without looking, as though she's ready for a Frenchman to kiss it. Our best time is ten fingers in under two minutes, so she has come quite a long way with the simple support of her mom being positive.

One day while our family was visiting the zoo, I received an ironic affirmation of my strong belief in positive terms. Lauren was sitting in her stroller and the rest of us were standing at a fence, looking at animals in the distance. Lauren indicated that she was thirsty, so Craig found the cup of water we had packed for her and handed it to her. At the same moment, I saw a stream of water just on the other side of the fence, so as Lauren took the cup from her dad, I said, "Oh, don't throw it in the water!" Almost before I could finish the sentence, Lauren heaved the cup through the air and over the fence. We all watched in awe as it made a splash and slowly floated downstream. Lauren was now without a drink and I'd just lost an expensive piece of Tupperware, a commodity which seems to disappear as quickly and mysteriously as socks in a dryer.

"Of all people, I can't believe you did that," Craig said to me in disbelief. "You told her to throw it in the water!"

"No, I told her, 'Don't throw it in the water!'" I clarified.

"And how often do you tell me not to do that? 'Tell what *to* do, not what *not* to do,' you always say." He shook his head in disbelief at me many times throughout the rest of the zoo visit. I was pretty embarrassed, but I kept pointing out to him what terrific evidence this was that I was right! When we tell a child "No" or "Don't" or "Stop," we're asking her to figure out on her own what behavior we prefer—the opposite of the negative behavior.

So, am I saying that you should never use the word "No"? *NO!* A few people have heard me consistently using positive terms with Lauren and have implied that she is a behavior problem because she doesn't hear the word "No." These people must not spend much time with me, as I've certainly been heard using the word "NO" quite loudly on multiple occasions. But I like to reserve that one for when there is no obvious positive way to say something. For example, when I caught Lauren dumping 200 ounces of liquid laundry detergent on my carpeting, I screamed, "NO!" loud enough to be heard three states away. In fact, I probably kept saying "No" as Craig bathed her and I scooped as much liquid as possible back into the bottle, knowing that the next few hours were now dedicated to cleaning the carpet of that which is most difficult to extract—anything which suds. (In this instance, saying "Keep Tide in the bottle" certainly wouldn't have communicated my meaning quite as well as an hysterical "NO!")

Certainly when Lauren is hurting someone who means her no harm, a "No!" or "Stop!" is more appropriate than a "Gentle" or "Hands Down." These are the few occasions that swift punishment is going to communicate the severity of her crime more appropriately than positively worded phrases. Lauren may not understand a "No" on this occasion any better than she normally would, but we must teach her that there are repercussions to her actions. She may not understand the specific meaning of "No," but only after consistent exposure will she learn that it's an indicator that she must stop what she's doing or face harsh consequences.

I actually prefer the word "Stop" to "No" as its meaning is more easily taught. Lauren and I have spent many hours playing "stop and go" games to teach her the meanings of these words. My favorite is to walk or run holding hands, then shout "Stop!" as we halt. In the early days, I would drag Lauren to a halt, but it didn't take her long to understand the rules of the game and to stop on her own. Of course, it was as much fun when I would start us up again with "Go!" We played this game crossing streets and walking across parking lots, just as other mothers do with their young children. (Though, I had extra incentive—my child would fly across the parking lot and never look back if I let go of that little hand.) The word "stop" seems more valuable than "no" when a child is about to step into a busy street, grab a hornets' nest from the side of a building, and probably when she is about to dump 200 ounces of liquid detergent on the carpeting, as well.

I not only believe there is a time and place for the word "no," I also believe we should teach our children to say "no" then respect them when they do. It's currently popular in the media to tell American children to "just say no" to a variety of ills in our society, but I've never seen a public service announcement about teaching non-verbal children how to say "no." For a child who uses sign language or understands abstract ideas conveyed on picture cards, this isn't so difficult. For a child who has never consistently shown understanding of abstract notions presented in any form, this instruction is a greater challenge. But the first way to teach "no" is to respect "no." If we offer Lauren something and she pushes it away, that's a clear indicator of "no." It's tempting to ignore her "no," particularly if we think that what we're offering is what she needs; but if we're not sure, we need to respect the "no."

I become frustrated at this scenario: I ask someone to show Lauren a choice of two favorite videos. Lauren pushes both choices away, so the person chooses one of the two for her and puts it in the VCR to play. "She chose that one?" I ask. "No," the person answers, "but she wouldn't choose one, so I chose for her." "She wouldn't look at them?"

I ask. "Yeah, she looked at them, but she pushed them both away," the person answers. "When you have no definite means of saying 'no,'" I explain, "pushing them both away is a 'no.'" Consistently after such a conversation, one of two things happens. I offer Lauren a choice of two entirely different videos and she clearly points to the one she wants. Or, Lauren leaves the room and we soon find out that she's not interested in a video because she's ill, hungry, or has some other very good reason. In other words, she proves to us that her "no" was truly a "no."

Craig and I like to reminisce about the first time he ate dinner at my parents' home. My dad asked, "How about more steak, Craig?" Craig answered, "No, thank you." My dad proceeded to put about one more pound of steak on his plate, saying, "You're a big guy, you can eat it." Craig was, of course, polite and ate as much of the steak as he could, but to this day, we're amused at my dad's complete disregard for his "no." We can laugh because we know that Dad's actions were an attempt to convey approval and generosity. But I bet Craig wouldn't be so amused if, after he married me, I ignored his "no" and put more food on his plate every time he said he was finished. Neurologically challenged or not, people can take only so much of "This is for your own good."

Receptive language (what a person understands) is important, but expressive language (what a person communicates) is equally important. It's the ability to express needs and wants (as well as knowing that those needs and wants will be respected and addressed) that empowers a person. Only when the basic need for security or peace of mind is met, may a person concern himself with higher level issues, such as improving his motor and cognitive skills. The ability to say "no" (verbally or non-verbally) is one important expressive language skill. The ability to make choices, at whatever level is meaningful to the individual, is another. Both skills may need to be taught. But don't bother teaching choice-making if you aren't going to respect the choices made.

Not long ago, I realized a benefit to using a schedule beyond helping to predict, plan and keep on track. After a year and a half of slow and steady progress in occupational therapy, Lauren started becoming angry and aggressive during sessions. Her loving therapist had told me week after week of the difficulties they were having when I spent one ride home thinking about what could be upsetting Lauren. I imagined that after the first difficult session, the therapist (O.T.) probably began subsequent sessions a little tense and expecting a fight. I thought of how things are at home when Lauren is upset and we're wearied of her challenging behavior; her anxiety spirals as it feeds off ours. Tensions are guaranteed to escalate until we introduce something new on which to focus. I thought about what I would do if I were the O.T. Then I telephoned her with my ideas.

The following week, the O.T. implemented all of my suggestions. The first order of business was to take the focus off Lauren and her behavior. Lauren consistently becomes anxious and unresponsive in testing situations, or in any situation where someone is observing her and simply waiting to see what she'll do next. It's a form of performance anxiety that I've mentioned elsewhere in this book. The first moment Lauren didn't cooperate (which was during the first minute of therapy during very bad sessions) the focus naturally shifted from the activity at hand to her behavior.

In order to provide other places for the therapist to focus, as well as for Lauren, we created a picture schedule. (Teachers often introduce such schedules to help children predict and plan, but therapists ordinarily do not because their time with the child is so limited.) This schedule's purpose was manifold. First and foremost, the schedule gave the O.T. something to discuss and draw Lauren's focus toward, instead of her behavior and performance. Written into the schedule were two helps specific to this goal. The first item on the schedule was *Take off shoes*. Because Lauren often took her shoes off even before entering the therapy room, listing this as a primary goal insured Lauren's success and a reason for praise at the start of each session. The second item on the schedule was *Play Music*. We had never played background music during this therapy before, but the O.T. was happy and agreeable to it upon hearing of its benefits at home. Not only might it help Lauren stay calm and focused, but it would also give the therapist something to talk about other than Lauren's behavior.

Because the O.T. didn't do exactly the same activities each week, we came up with a schedule that listed activities in a general fashion: *Hand time* stood for whatever fine-motor task they would do, as all these activities involved the hands. *Ball/Bouncing Time* stood for a variety of activities that included balls. Every session ended with time for Lauren to swing on one of a number of different types of swings, so *Swing Time* was the final item. This type of schedule also empowered Lauren by allowing her choices within each category. For example, she could choose between two familiar fine-motor activities during *Hand Time*, or choose the type of swing she wanted to swing on that day during *Swing Time*. Though she has no choice about being in therapy, having choice within her schedule gives her some control over her own life. I imagine I would be uncooperative if I had no control over all the activity being thrust upon me, so we try to offer Lauren control and choice whenever possible.

Like any schedule, this one also served the purpose of helping Lauren predict and plan. This is especially important when she finds an activity aversive. The therapist is consistent in their activities and the repeated exposure teaches Lauren what she must accomplish to make an activity end. This schedule also gave control back to the therapist. If an adult gives up on a task a child can't accomplish because she's upset, it may give the child a sense of having gained control of the situation. With a schedule in hand, the therapist appears in control of whether a task will be required on a particular day. When she announces the level of effort she expects before it's time to move on to the next activity, the adult maintains control. (Expressions like "taking control" are often used in derogatory ways to describe misbehaving children. I don't equate a child gaining control with a child getting his or her way. Most children I know don't want control and don't know what to do with it when an adult hands it over. That's where the misbehavior comes in. They would much rather an adult be their guide, as they don't have the knowledge or maturity to make such decisions comfortably.)

The first week Lauren's O.T. began using the new schedule, Lauren's behavior completely changed. She was immediately cooperative and showed no signs of the aggression we had seen for many weeks, right up to the previous session. Each week, Lauren became more loving to her therapist, obviously appreciative of being respected and of all the opportunities for success built into the schedule. Lauren responded particularly well to the new opportunities for choice-making. Her O.T. often commented after a session that she was pleasantly surprised when Lauren made a choice of activity different from what she expected. This new information helped her to understand what was causing some of Lauren's previous frustration—she didn't like to do many of the activities her therapist thought were favorites!

A few years ago, Craig and I witnessed the use of a picture communication system that looked in many ways similar to those Lauren used at the time. In practice, however, it was very different. We were touring special education classrooms to check out the offerings of the public school system. In one classroom with a ratio of two teachers to two students, Craig and I were impressed until the speech therapist came in for one little girl's therapy time. The therapist set up a large display of a variety of pictures that apparently held meaning for the girl. The two sat at a table across from each other and the adult handed her a favorite stim object. After a minute, the woman took the stimmy away and told the girl to get the picture of what she wanted. She got the picture of the stimmy off the board, handed it to the woman and received the stim item back. The woman put the picture back on the board and this sequence recurred a few more times when the woman told her again to get the picture of what she wanted. This time, the girl walked to the board, perused it carefully, picked up a picture of a juice box, walked back to the woman and gave it to her. I was impressed after all! The girl had independently made a request!

"No, no, that's not what you want." the therapist responded, walking up to the board and putting the card back. She sat back down, seeming a little flustered and said again, "Show me what you want."

The student obediently walked back to the board and, quicker than the last time, chose the juice box picture, walked back to the table and handed it to the woman. The woman looked at the picture in frustration. I couldn't restrain myself any longer and I said quietly, but loud enough for the therapist to hear, "Perhaps she's thirsty and truly wants some juice."

The woman said to a teacher in the room, "I don't have any juice with me. She usually doesn't pick juice." Craig and I looked at each other simultaneously, eyes wide. "Why would she have any choice on that board that she doesn't have with her?!" we both wondered silently. The reason soon became clear.

"She usually wants pudding," she whispered to the teacher. I wasn't sure if this therapist believed that children with communication disabilities never became thirsty, or if she just walked into this classroom with no expectations of expressive communication from this little girl that day. The teacher brought in a cup of water and the therapist opened a cup of chocolate pudding, but the girl was interested in neither. I couldn't help but be sad for a long time about the missed opportunity for reinforcement. I wondered if that little girl was ever again motivated to express her desires to this woman, and whether the therapist, having learned from her mistake, had the appropriate reward and praise ready for the next opportunity.

It's easy for me to see the error of the ways of this speech therapist, but I must admit that sometimes I miss or ignore an obvious expressive communication overture from my own daughter. Just a few weeks ago, Lauren was looking for a snack in the refrigerator and in all the kitchen cabinets. (I normally offer Lauren photo choices of foods at snack time, but this particular day, the cabinets were literally bare. There seems to be a consistent correlation between a lack of food in my house, and my lack of desire to set foot in a grocery store.) Finally, Lauren seemed satisfied with a choice. She pulled on a corner of a bag of chocolate chips on the lowest shelf in the cupboard until it plopped onto the counter. She carried the bag to the dining room, set it on the table, then pulled her chair out and sat in front of the bag. She fondled the bag expectantly as I explained that Mom bought that bag to make cookies. "I know what you really want is cookies," I told her as I slipped the bag from in front of her. "OK, I'll make some cookies now," I decided and said in the same instant to relieve my guilt.

About two hours later (baking is a complicated task in our house—it necessitates a lack of Lauren supervision, which frequently results in some side chores requiring the vacuum cleaner, steam cleaner and/or bathtub) the cookies were done. I pulled the first batch out of the oven, let them cool on a rack for a few minutes, then handed Bryn and Lauren one cookie each to bring to the table. When I joined them with a cookie of my own, Bryn was giggling. "You're on a chip excursion, aren't you, Lauren?" she said. The table directly in front of Lauren did, in fact, look like an anthropological dig site. The pieces of cookie (which was now hundreds of crumbs) that had once surrounded each chocolate chip had been carefully pulled and brushed off each chip, then pushed to the side. As she succeeded in locating and fully exposing each single chip, Lauren carefully put it in her mouth, then started on the next suspect piece of cookie.

"Lauren, I guess when you say you want chocolate chips, you mean you want chocolate chips, not chocolate chip cookies." Lauren just looked up at me with a smile. I pointed out a missed chip in a small chunk of cookie then went into the kitchen to get more. I thought about how relatively calm Lauren had been during the baking process. As I handed her another cookie to excavate, I said, "Thank you, Lauren, for so patiently waiting for Mommy to repackage the chips."

Laughter

My mom and I have recently gotten into the habit of sending each other an e-mail every evening. We've always had a close relationship, but she now lives over one thousand miles from me, so this has been a nice way of sharing even the little moments with each other. The other day I was typing away about my day, which included a trip with my daughters to the market for produce:

We went to the farmer's market today and Lauren walked behind the grocery cart and pushed it. She picked out some apples for me and put some in a bag. When I told her once, "Let me just go and get a bag" she dashed off in the other direction and I thought she was trying to escape, but then she stopped at a different roll of bags that we had just passed. She was getting a bag like I said!

A grapefruit fell out of the cart and rolled across the floor. She went running after it. When she got to it, she picked it up and I said, "Thank you, Lauren, now bring it here, so we can put it in the bag." She took it and whacked it on the floor about five times, then brought it over to me. Gee, thanks, I thought, but I put it in the bag. I figured it was pretty obvious that, yes, we're the ones who bruised this one. Most people would put it back because they bruised it unintentionally, but any onlookers would have realized that we're premeditated serial bruisers.

I was amused at the time of the grapefruit bashing, but ever since my mom told me how much my dad and she laughed over that story, it's become part of Lauren-lore. Lauren-lore is any story about Lauren that, every now and then, is retold with an intro of "Remember when…" Sometimes the details are fuzzy, so Craig, Bryn and I compare versions to get an accurate account. Unless, of course, I knew it was Lauren-lore the moment it happened and took the wise measure of writing down an account immediately. Unfortunately, with mothering and teaching as first priorities, hundreds of Lauren-lore stories have only been preserved in the oral tradition. Even the stories that weren't necessarily funny when they occurred seem to have an eye-opening, ironic or outright funny ending in the retelling.

Some Lauren-lore never really happened. I've had many dreams about Lauren that were probably meant to tell me more about myself than Lauren, but the humor in them makes them Lauren-lore. When Lauren was a toddler and not speaking at all, I had the most memorable dream I have ever had. In it, I was driving my car and Lauren was sitting in the back seat. Another driver cut me off, and I loudly said something very nasty—"You far gone ash mule!" (No, those weren't the real words, but you get the picture.) Within an instant, I heard Lauren's voice in the back seat echo, "You far gone ash mule!" I turned around in shock and shouted, "You talked!" Then added, "Don't ever say those words again!"

I woke up immediately in a panic. "Is it true? Did Lauren talk?" I asked myself as I figured out where I was. When I realized that it was entirely a dream and that Lauren had not said those words, I was disappointed and relieved at the same time.

God may very well have planted that dream in my head as a reminder of the example I'm setting for my children. (I like to think my driving behavior has improved as a result, but...I'm always trying.) If so, He planted it with the irony built right in. If nothing else, Lauren's autism has assured me of one thing. God has the best sense of humor and He loves for us to be in on the joke.

One day, I was dealing with very difficult behavior from Lauren, while also trying to get too many things done. It was a hot day, so I filled a kiddy pool with water and put it in our front yard, a few feet from the bottom step to our porch. Lauren loved playing in water, so I knew she wouldn't run. Bryn kept an eye on her with an occasional check-in from me. After awhile, Bryn came running into the house almost crying because there were bees flying nearby. Knowing Bryn is extremely fearful of bees, I told her to calm down. Then I gave her a familiar lecture about being brave, adding that if a bee came near her, she should just stand still until it flew away. "So, bees are not out to hurt you, right?" I ended, "And we're not going to freak out about them, right?" "Right," Bryn hesitantly agreed.

I went to check on Lauren who had been left by herself too long by then. As I walked through the front door, I saw her jumping as high as she could. Her arm and hand were outstretched and I saw a bee just barely escape her closing fist. She was trying to catch the fuzzy bees! "Danger! Danger!" I screamed. "Bees can hurt you!"

The irony hit me almost immediately. I turned around and Bryn was standing behind me. "Oh, yeah, Lauren was having fun trying to catch the bees," she said. I stayed on the porch nearby for the rest of this outside play time and accomplished little else the rest of the afternoon.

That same evening, despite my chuckle at the bee situation, I was still in a sour mood while driving to church for band practice. I was in Craig's car and the headlight knob did not want to stay in place. Every time I let go of it, the headlights would go off. I had to hold it in the *on* position for almost the entire trip to the church. When I arrived at the church, as soon as I slammed the locked car door behind me, I noticed something. The headlights were on. I remembered turning the knob to the *off* position, but now they didn't seem to want to go off. I would have been quite frustrated at having to set down all the stuff in my arms to unlock the car, but I couldn't escape the point. I felt like someone was standing behind me saying, "You have very funny children and a very funny car and all I'm trying to do is give you a sweet little chuckle to end your day. Take it." And I did. That little car is now gone, but its headlight knob never had a problem again after that evening.

The laughing in our house didn't start with the arrival of autism. (Though autism did increase our need and repertoire drastically.) The biggest reason Craig and I are together is probably our shared sense of humor. Craig, in particular, can see the funny side to almost anything. I've been awakened many mornings to good news that was good solely because of the presentation. For example: "Good morning. Before you go into the living room, I just want to warn you that Lauren's already been working on a school science project today. She performed an experiment to see if there was a bottom to the inside of that new Kleenex box you put out yesterday. The answer is…YES!"

Craig is the first one to recommend Downy fabric softener to friends who are looking for a good wood floor polisher. I wasn't home the night that Lauren dumped a bottle of it in the room with the most beat up hardwood floor in the house. Craig told me on the phone that he was tempted to dump a second bottle on the other half of the room, as the side he cleaned up is now so much nicer looking. I've asked him not to do it many times, though I think he's serious, not just covering for his daughter.

I remember the first time after Lauren was diagnosed that we laughed about autism. Craig has put on some magic shows for young children's birthday parties in the past and one of his favorite dreams is to be a professional clown. Lauren was often in her own little world at that time and, sometimes while in this state, she would start laughing for no reason apparent to the rest of us. This particular evening, Lauren was sitting in her high chair in the dining room. All of a sudden, she began laughing. Her head was tilted to the side so that all she could see was the wall, which was covered with a brown leafy wallpaper. Bryn, Craig and I couldn't help but chuckle at Lauren's delight in something we couldn't see, particularly as one of the few times we heard her voice was when she laughed. After a few minutes of listening to on-and-off laughter, Craig stood up and announced, "I could be a clown for kids with autism!" He went over to the wall and dramatically gestured with hands wide toward the wall. Lauren laughed her loudest. "Maybe I could cut big squares of this paper off the wall and just flash it for the same effect."

I said, "Craig!" in an attempt to act appropriately indignant at his politically incorrect comments about what would humor a population with this disability. But I couldn't stop chuckling. I think I realized right then that there was nothing politically correct about autism. Besides, it felt so good to laugh about a subject that we had only spent many hours sobbing about until then.

A few years ago, I came up with a new theory about Lauren's disability. Lauren had taken a sudden interest in a children's show on our PBS station. It was a puppet show named *Salsa* which was entirely in Spanish. I watched Lauren one day as she came running into the room when the theme song starting playing, and as she sat the entire half hour mesmerized. When Craig came home that evening, I joyfully proclaimed, "Our problems are over!" When he looked at me curiously, I explained, "Lauren doesn't have autism. She was just born speaking Spanish!"

Humor has gotten me through so many days and has probably been responsible for my children putting up with me as well. Lauren has always liked dried leaves and pine straw (probably for their stim value) but one particular autumn, she seemed absolutely in love with them. We get little to no snow where we live, so this infatuation was still present at Christmas-time when I sat down to write our family's annual newsletter. I began:

It's hard to believe it's December when Lauren just developed a leaf fetish—she's enjoying romping in, dancing with, and all around cavorting with dried-up leaves and pine straw, wherever we go. So, we're thanking God we don't typically get snow this time of year. Leaf romping is easy and free entertainment every afternoon. (Though it's tough when Craig tries to pull a load of raked up leaves to the road. Lauren implies, "Let my people go!" as she hosts sit-in after sit-in on the plastic Craig tries to drag from the back yard. So far, she's been quite successful for the cause.)

When the weather became too cold and wet to take the children outside most afternoons, Lauren still begged to go outside. When she wasn't staring out the window at the bounty on the ground (I don't think we raked until spring that year) she was trying to communicate in every way possible that she wanted to go outside. She dragged me to the door again and again. She cried. She carried everyone's shoes and jackets to the door. It was an adorable and pitiful sight. One day, I picked her up to hug her through her sadness. I wanted to make her aware that I knew what she wanted and that I sympathized with her disappointment. I came up with the blues-iest sounding tune I could think of and sang her this song:

> My name is Lauren and I love my leaves.
> I want to go outside, so please let me, please!
> My name is Lauren...
> And I want to go outside...
> My name is Lauren...
> And I want to go outside...

I put one of Lauren's arms around my waist and held the other. Then I bounced her on my hip while we looked out the window and I sang. Lauren loved it, especially when I dipped her. As I tired and the song ended, she'd bounce and push my hand back and forth to get me started again. We had Bryn singing, dancing and laughing, too. What a treat to, at least once in my life, replace a sorrowful moment with a silly one!

An even earlier fetish of Lauren's seemed to be an offshoot of her general love of circles, big and small. She liked to place small objects in a circular fashion. For a while, when we gave her dry Cheerios or popcorn, she would spread the pieces out in a line, then push the line away from her until it formed an arch shape on the table. Craig and I joked that all pieces were equidistant from her hand that way. One day, Lauren dumped a basket full of tiny toys. She sat in the middle of them, then pushed them all away from her until there was an almost perfect circle of toys surrounding her. Craig was watching and called me into the room. As I walked in, he said, "Look! Toyhenge!"

Of course, conversation at that point turned to possible explanations for Stonehenge. Perhaps some ruler with autism dictated the building of the phenomenon, or maybe some aliens with autism. And then there are crop *circles*...

Though laughter may be a coping mechanism for Craig and me, I believe it's also our most important means of creating a positive environment in our home. Even if I do everything I can to respect, empathize with and empower Lauren, there are moments, as well as entire days, when nothing goes right and Lauren is a very upset child. Being able to step away from the situation and see some humor in it brings us out from the depths of anger or sorrow time and time again. I don't know how I would repeatedly call it a new day and step right back into the ring without my husband or daughter regularly giving me a reason to smile first.

The other day, I was headed out the door, late for an appointment, racing around gathering things I would need, becoming more stressed as each minute passed. Craig had kindly put Lauren in the car on his way to the shed for something. Bryn came inside and announced, "I started the car, but Lauren's taken her clothes off." There are few things I dislike more than dressing an unwilling child in the back seat of the car, particularly when it's very cold or rainy outside, as it was that day.

"Tell Daddy to redress her then!" I yelled back, wondering how much later this would make us. I was finally ready to walk out the door when Craig walked in.

"Lauren took her clothes off," he said.

"You redressed her, didn't you?" I asked in panic.

"Yes," he said, "and I couldn't blame her for stripping." I looked at him questioningly and he explained with a straight face, "When I leaned into the car to gather her clothes, I realized that Rush Limbaugh was on the radio. I strip every time I hear Rush, too."

Once again, Craig saved the trip to this particular appointment. I tried to remain irritated, but I kept picturing Craig unconsciously unbuttoning his shirt upon the start of every Rush Limbaugh show. When I got into the car, Lauren was still dressed. I turned to her and said, "Hooray! I hear Bryn switched the radio to music for you!" I'm not sure if Lauren expected me to be angry about the stripping, but she seemed very pleased when a happy Mom got into the car.

In the beginning of this chapter, I mentioned my daily e-mail exchange with my mom. For some reason, we have always signed off our e-mails with "Love you more than…" For example, "Love you more than all the fish in all the water in the world" or "Love you more than all the words I've ever typed on this keyboard." (I think it started when I quoted my younger sister. When she was a preschooler and I was in college, she would say goodbye to me at the end of each weekend visit with "Love you more than dinosaurs weigh." It tickles me to think that was the greatest amount she could think of and that was how much she loved me.) Upon looking at the grapefruit story e-mail for this chapter, I noticed how I signed off that evening:

Love you more than all the tears we've shed and all the prayers we've said, and all the laughs we've had because of Lauren,

Nannette

Family, Friends and Strangers

I would never have met half of the coolest people I know if it weren't for Lauren. That's a fact. Some of my favorite people are therapists, doctors, teachers and moms of children with autism whom I never would have met if Lauren didn't have autism. I've never analyzed why these people tend to draw my admiration. Perhaps the complex nature of autism is a clue. Those interested in autism are likely complex individuals, and I find complexity interesting. There's also nobility inherent in much of the work of helping people with autism. An autistic person's unpredictable or aggressive behavior can be confusing, upsetting and even frightening. Addressing such behavior is not a job for the faint-hearted. It is a job for a person with a sacrificial spirit and strong sense of self. These are the sort of people with whom I like to spend my time.

Because we live about one thousand miles from most of our relatives, they don't have an opportunity to get to know Lauren the way many of our friends do. Craig's and my circle of friends is like family. If we have to run a child to the hospital in the middle of the night, we'll call a nearby friend who is here and able to help rather than a relative. We stay close to our daughters' grandparents through visits, e-mail and phone calls, but we stay in the town we're in because this feels like home.

I believe Lauren's autism has been a draw to people with big hearts. We've collected them over the years: volunteers who helped with Lauren's program in the early days; people who have called out of the blue to offer help; members of our church who would see Lauren on Sundays and stop to say hello to her, taking her hand and waiting on a response; doctors who save me magazine articles about new treatments and hand them to me saying, "It might help her, don't you think!?"

Our hairdresser first came into our lives when I could no longer cut Lauren's hair. In the early days when I just needed to trim her wispy baby hair, I could sit Lauren in front of a favorite Sesame Street video and clip away. When the sight and sound of scissors began to send her into a panic, I started sneaking into Lauren's bedroom at night to trim her hair. Thankfully, she looked great in short layers. They're easier to make look straight after doing one side at a time—flipping the sleeping child over in between. When Lauren started waking up during haircut time, I needed to call in a professional. A friend recommended a hairdresser who had come to her house to cut her child's hair. Kirsten came to our house and was very loving to Lauren. Lauren hated having her hair cut and fought the entire process, but she hugged and smiled at Kirsten before and after the haircut. When we set up a dining room chair in the kitchen, Lauren would drag the chair back out, thereby insisting that no haircut was going to happen if she had any say about it. But once the bangs were trimmed, the back was neat and the floor was swept, Lauren would drag Kirsten to her bedroom to show off and giggle.

After a few home appointments, our entire family began going to Kirsten's shop for haircuts. Sometimes Lauren is cooperative and hardly needs a hand on her knee to keep still while she looks at herself in the mirror. Other times, her dad and I must situate ourselves like human vise grips around her body, holding her hands down. But every time, Kirsten is calm and reassuring, telling Lauren what a great job she's doing and how beautiful she looks. Even when Lauren throws her head suddenly and Kirsten nicks her own hand with the scissors, there's no wince or sign of frustration, just more reassurances. That this woman is also a talented hairdresser is an unbelievable blessing!

One of Lauren's Sunday School teachers, Jeanne, told me when I first met her that she didn't know much about autism, but she loved children and had experience helping in a special ed classroom. After over a year of being with Lauren most Sunday afternoons, Jeanne nervously told me she wanted to stop helping with the Sunday School class. (I knew she was under a lot of stress while starting up an at-home business as a full-time artist, so her announcement didn't take me by surprise.) Jeanne said she would still like to come over to our house to watch Bryn and Lauren from time to time. I've taken her up on her offer a few times (particularly when Lauren's behavior hadn't been good for a while) when we needed to attend something important, such as Bryn's first piano recital. Jeanne had many Sundays of experience dealing with Lauren when she wasn't feeling well or when her behavior was inexplicably atrocious, so I knew she could handle herself in more challenging scenarios than our usual babysitters could.

One day, I called Jeanne last minute to ask if she could stay with the girls for two hours while Craig and I joined some friends for a gathering. She said, "yes," and Craig and I went out that evening. When we returned, I found Jeanne in Lauren's room. Lauren was being coy under some blankets, giggling and acting like the whole evening had been nonstop merriment for everyone. It was only after talking with Jeanne (while being interrupted by Bryn a few times with announcements like, "Lauren pulled Jeanne's hair!") that I found out how much Jeanne had endured without complaint. When she left, Craig turned to me and asked, "Where'd we find her?" "I have no idea," I said, "I'm just glad we did."

Elizabeth came into our lives when she was ten years old. I had placed an ad in a homeschooling newsletter for a girl fourteen or older who could watch Lauren in my home while I took Bryn to her dance lesson only two miles away. (Having Lauren in the community center where Bryn's lessons took place had become quite a challenge. Most Tuesday afternoons, I was fighting tears by the time I picked Bryn up from the dance room—I was often scolded by center staff when Lauren would get away from me and run through the facility. I had to run after her or I would have lost her, so I appeared as impudent as my child.) Two girls over fourteen called and one actually came over to spend a little time with Lauren, but she never returned. (She was very quiet and did not interest Lauren in the least.) When Elizabeth called, I answered the phone and heard, "I know your ad said fourteen and older, but I'll be eleven in a few weeks and I love children!" (Elizabeth already helped out regularly with her four younger brothers and sisters at home. I guess she wanted a greater childcare challenge!)

Elizabeth is sixteen as I write this and has brought our family more joy than we could have imagined. Despite her hectic schedule, and the fact that Bryn no longer takes dance lessons, Elizabeth comes over for about four hours just about every Friday to help out with Lauren. Her unpaid job description is "mother's helper" but "undecorated angel" or "restorer of deteriorating spirits" would be more accurate. She has never hesitated to help Lauren in the bathroom, and she was the first person to put Lauren to bed at night while Craig and I were out on a rare date. Of course, her family members have become our friends; they're obviously special people to have raised such a daughter. This is one of those lifelong relationships that will exist despite Elizabeth's probable future of college, work and a family. She is family to us. She's one of the rare jewels that almost make Craig and me thankful for Lauren's autism, as I can't imagine how we would have met Elizabeth without it.

It may sound like encountering a special needs child necessarily brings out the best in a person, but this isn't true for everyone. The three women I just mentioned are exceptionally empathetic and giving people. Out of deep-seated compassion, they strive to understand Lauren. Because they put in the effort, they understand how difficult Lauren's challenges are and that helps them see past her behavior. I strive to keep only such people in my life, but some people who aren't as compassionate are unavoidable.

My first rule of thumb for negative people is *Ditch 'em!* Life is too short and too difficult to spend any more time than necessary with people who bring me or my family down. I live according to this rule not because I believe such people have no redeeming value. (My mother worked hard to instill in me that "we love everyone on this earth. We may hate a person's actions, but we must try to love the person.") It's simply because my plate is full and I must prioritize. Time spent nurturing a hurtful relationship would be time *not* spent trying to heal my daughter and keep my family whole, so I can't dedicate such time. I have time only to remember these people in prayer and hope that others will address their needs.

Lauren is very sensitive to the disapproval, discomfort, anxiety or anger of others. I try to avoid such people at all cost. When we can't avoid them, I help Lauren to predict and plan for the occasion as much as possible. Then I try to keep the environment and emotions as calm as possible. Finally, if the person is still negative or hurtful, I try to remember always to be my child's advocate. Even if it will add to the disturbance, I think it's better for Lauren to hear her mom defend her honor, intentions or motivation than just to walk away with no such show of support. I don't know how much Lauren understands, but I hope she knows that her mom will let no one hurt her children unchecked on her watch.

Sometimes, negativity shows up in surprising places. Craig and I have encountered people who think the Special Olympics are unfair to their developmentally normal children, because they aren't allowed to participate. I remember a conversation between Bryn and me when she was about six years old. She said to me, "It's not fair that Lauren gets to go to therapy all the time. I wish I could go to therapy." I told her I understood why she'd want to go to therapy. Lauren received all the attention at therapy and her therapists were so nice. Then I reminded her that she took dance lessons, could ride a bicycle, play team sports and go over to friends' houses to play. "Lauren goes to therapy because she can't do those sorts of things," I said. "Would you want to give up those things to be like Lauren and go to therapy instead?"

"No way!" Bryn quickly answered. The discrepancy between Lauren's "opportunities" and her own were immediately obvious to Bryn at six years old, but they weren't obvious to the adults who complained

about the Special Olympics. I can (almost) understand someone feeling left out from a life experience that someone else obviously enjoys.
However, I also understand that if these people gave of their time to
others with greater challenges than their own, they would likely walk
away from the experience with at least as much joy as the people they
set out to help.

I listen to Dr. Laura Schlessinger's radio talk show often when I'm
in the car. (Lauren doesn't usually like talk radio, with the exception of
Dr. Laura. Lauren even seems comforted by the sound of Dr. Laura's
voice.) Dr. Laura has taught me a few useful life lessons. Whenever
someone calls in to complain about a friend or relative's behavior, Dr.
Laura asks, "Is this the first time that this person has behaved this way
or does he often act this way?" The person invariably responds, "Oh,
yes, this person has always been unreasonable (nasty/a gossiper/what-
ever the case may be)." To which Dr. Laura replies, "Then why are you
surprised (or upset)? He is just acting completely as you expect him to
act."

When a friend or relative says something purposefully discouraging
or treats Lauren as sub-human, Craig tells me about it with great frustration and disbelief. I've gotten into the habit of asking him, "Is it surprising that the person did this or does he have a history of such
behavior?" The person always has a memorable "criminal record," so I
respond with, "And you're surprised by this behavior…why…?" Somehow, pointing out the person's predictable pattern of misbehavior
helps us to let go of the incident and leave it where it belongs—in the
pile of evidence that we should limit our exposure to the person as he is
unlikely to change.

Craig and I have some relatives and friends who express concern
from time to time about Bryn and how living with a sister with autism
affects her. From my thorough observation of my older daughter, I can
attest to her strong character, her terrific sense of humor, and the fact
that she enjoys time spent with her family more than any other time. I
attended a one-day workshop years ago about siblings of children with

disabilities. Grown siblings were there on a panel to share their experience and answer questions. What I learned from this event seemed to me to be a whole lot of common sense. I learned that children growing up with a disabled sibling tend to be more mature and nurturing than other children. There was concern expressed by the presenters that taking on too much of a care-taking role as a child was a negative thing, but the panel of grown-up siblings never mentioned that as a problem. They each discussed similar concerns: that people treat their brothers or sisters with respect, and that *parents* of disabled children take time away for *them*selves. These were some of the most caring and intelligent-sounding young adults I have ever seen assembled. The goal of the workshop leaders seemed to be to worry the parents in attendance about the adverse effects one child's disability could have on the lives of their other offspring. On the contrary, I left this workshop feeling reassured that all Craig and I have to do is pay attention to Bryn's needs, and she's going to turn out just fine.

To those who suggest Bryn's existence is less than it could be because Lauren's disability limits our ability to vacation, for example, or because she has to endure gluten and casein-free foods, I tell them, "Don't tell Bryn how bad everything is because she's under the illusion that she's very happy." Craig and I take turns taking Bryn out for pizza or dinner at a restaurant, or to the bookstore, library or movies, calling these "Daddy/Daughter dates" or "Mommy/Daughter dates." Sometimes, special time is as easy as letting Bryn stay up past Lauren's bedtime so we can order in pizza, play a family game or watch a movie that Lauren would not like. I think Bryn feels a little guilty that Lauren doesn't get all this attention. One night, upon arriving home from a date with me at a restaurant, she walked over to Lauren to say "hello," rubbed her sister's head and said, "I think next time is Lauren's turn to go on a Mommy/Daughter date. I don't think she's ever been on one!"

As Lauren grows older, my biggest concern for Bryn is how often our house is a stressful place because of the latest challenging behaviors. However, for all people, what is common becomes normalcy. I remember when Bryn was seven or eight years old and Lauren was throwing an angry fit. I was trying to calm her down and it was becoming quite an episode. Suddenly, Bryn appeared. I could see her mouth moving and could almost make out over the racket that she was telling me about something she had read or wanted to show me an outfit she had concocted for her Barbie doll. I asked her loudly if she really thought this was a good time, with Lauren whining and fighting me. Bryn's expression changed, as though she suddenly saw Lauren and noticed that she was, in fact, screaming and in a tantrum. She walked out of the room to await the end of the scene, when I would be better able to listen to her.

I told Craig about it when he came home from work. "It was as though I was doing something really obvious, like wrestling an alligator, and someone came up to me and nonchalantly asked, 'What would you like for Easter dinner this year, ham or turkey?'" I realized that day that even though my dealings with Lauren are often fraught with emotion and feel as out of the ordinary to me as wrestling an alligator, to Bryn, they're the status quo. She's never known anything different. Hopefully, this means that her blood pressure doesn't increase with every new challenge the way mine does!

I think the greatest evidence that Bryn is happy with her life has come, time and again, directly from the "mouths of babes." When Bryn was nine years old, Craig and I were talking at the dinner table about some significant progress Lauren had recently made. Bryn was quiet, then suddenly spoke up, sounding a little upset. "I just can't imagine Lauren talking. I don't want her to talk," she said. When I asked why, she answered, "She wouldn't be Lauren. She's so sweet the way she is." This wasn't the first time Bryn had shooed the idea of Lauren improving too drastically.

Maybe such conversations are just evidence of children accepting the status quo as normalcy. Bryn doesn't like the idea of change whenever we tell her it's coming, but she consistently embraces change as soon as she realizes how it will benefit her. That she can't imagine the benefit to her sister speaking and not having autism is quite a commentary on her view of her own life. It must not be so shabby.

Just as some people are concerned for Bryn (for some right reasons and some wrong ones) so do many express their concern for Craig and me having time together, away from responsibility. "Do you ever get time away for yourselves?" many friends have asked. They easily see the obvious—how our family is lacking in opportunity compared to families without a disabled child. And they're right. We do miss out on many forms of rest and recreation that most families enjoy.

We're very appreciative when concerned friends take action and offer to babysit. Babysitting Lauren involves an extensive orientation, so these people are sacrificing significant time out of their lives. This is a gift that can never be repaid. I always hope these friends experience some of the unpredictable, joy-filled moments that happen around Lauren. These moments are a huge blessing to me, so hopefully they serve as appropriate thanks for such generosity. Some of these babysitting friends have received more hugs and kisses from Lauren than I ever have, so I imagine they've experienced at least a few moments of "Lauren-joy." (They keep coming back!)

It's great to get away for a while—individually, or two to three of us at a time without Lauren. But if that were a constant focus—if we equated fun with escape—we probably would feel more burdened when we were not away. That's why I invest most of my time trying to create a positive environment and a positive schedule for all four of us. Those of us on the inside for the day-in and day-out work of raising Lauren might be missing out on what some other people get to enjoy, but we're also sure to be there for the unexpected moments of joy that turn into impromptu celebrations.

Jeanne had a lot of questions about Lauren and about autism the night she babysat for us. (Her interest grows as a relative is now raising a child with autism.) Jeanne asked me if I minded when she told me about her relative's experiences with autism. I honestly told her I appreciated anybody's sincere interest in the topic. Even with strangers or acquaintances, questions are always better than blank stares, or that squinty-eyed look of someone who ordinarily has something intelligent to say, but is taken completely off guard by the unusual topic (Craig and I are notorious for creating awkward lulls in conversation at social gatherings.)

Craig and I have compared notes on what we've found to be the most common things said to us in conversations where Lauren's disability becomes the topic. (Other people struggling with severe disability or illness tell me they hear these same things often.) The first is some variation of "Wow, you're an amazing person. I could never do what you do." When spoken by a friend who knows my circumstances well, I try to humbly accept these words as the compliment they're intended to be. Sometimes, however, a person says this in order to quickly end the conversation while walking away. This type of response starts me questioning the statements' validity and has often led me to theorize. Now when I hear these words, I consistently fight the urge to grab the person by the shoulder, spin him around and ask, "Are you really saying that if you had a child with autism, you wouldn't do everything in your power to help her live an independent and fulfilling life? Are you suggesting that you would love a child with autism less than you say you love your other children?" When these comments are made for the purpose of nipping conversation in the bud, however, Craig and I don't get the opportunity to interrogate. The fact of the matter is that we have no special powers which enable us to handle the many challenges of autism without becoming discouraged and occasionally depressed. I don't know why some people want to believe we do.

The second thing most commonly said is: "God doesn't give you anything you can't handle." I've come up with a reply to this one: "If that were true, there would be no children in institutions." Almost all people who say this one do so while walking quickly away. They seem to want us to understand that God has given us what it takes to raise this child and to be happy about it. Perhaps this is a safety against needing to express compassion. (Compassion seems to be an uncomfortable emotion for some people.) It certainly eliminates the need to continue to think about our complicated situation—God's taken care of us, after all.

In fact, God does give us above and beyond what we can handle. That's the only way we'll become uncomfortable enough to seek Him and to gain the ultimate reward of eternal life with Him. But this idea is challenging to express in the time allotted at the water cooler or in a grocery store check-out line, so I usually let people slide when their comments are one of the top two.

Lauren exhibits many behaviors that elicit questions from people. It would be nice to have all the answers. Parents of normally developing children do have answers to most questions posed to them about their children. "Does she like ballet?" "Will he be taking soccer again in the fall?" "What's her favorite subject in school?" These are all pretty easy questions to answer. Craig and I are often asked questions like, "Why is she doing that?" or "What's the matter with her?"

Craig and I have a running joke with each other. (Actually, it's more something I do that annoys him.) When Lauren's behavior brings about a question like, "What's bothering her?" Craig will try to answer with his best guess: "There are too many people here" or "The bright lights are probably bothering her" or "I think she's having a reaction to some gluten she had today." Then I interrupt and say, "Actually, we don't know." Craig's and my guesses at why Lauren's behavior is as it is are only guesses. When we tell someone confidently what is "the matter" with Lauren, she often disproves us anyway. If we say, "This music must be bothering her," Lauren may calm down before the music ever changes. Or she may escort the inquiring person to the door as an obvious statement that he or she is provoking the anxiety, so please leave!

I credit Ann Donnellan, author and educator in the fields of rehabilitation psychology and special education, with first giving me the confidence to say "I don't know." I attended a conference at which Dr. Donnellan was a speaker. One of the first things she said to the parents and professionals in attendance was, "The most important thing I want you to leave with today is the ability to say 'I don't know.' Repeat after me: 'I don't know.'" I believe the attendees practiced saying "I don't know" about three or four times to make us all feel comfortable with the fact that we can't know exactly what's going on in the minds and lives of the people with autism we're trying to help. There's a natural inclination to want to have answers to questions posed by family, friends and strangers. But if we're honestly doing all we can to heal, love and reach our daughter, the good people who witness our work day-in and day-out will accept an "I don't know" and stand by us until the day we do have all the answers.

To Church or Not to Church

A mong all the ways autism affects people, I believe it affects my family the most spiritually. That's a pretty big statement, as the physical effects (you probably realize by now) are obvious and incalculable. But when autism entered my worldview, it changed everything.

I was a content sofa Catholic before Lauren was diagnosed. I went to church every Sunday that it didn't conflict with other plans and I believed most of what was handed down to me by my mom, whose Catholic faith was handed her by her own parents. My mom and grandparents were not only devout in their faith, they were also sincere. My mom began actively reading and trying to apply the Bible to her life when I was young, so that was also my intention as I embarked on the early days of marriage and child rearing.

My family had become very active in our local church by the time Lauren was diagnosed. In fact, Craig went through the year-long preparation class and became Catholic that same year. Until Lauren was three years old, we were able to attend Mass and participate in some family church activities without a problem. We stopped going to church as a family when Lauren started crawling beneath pews as soon as we sat down. She would physically fight Craig and me when we tried to force her to stay with us in our pew. I didn't blame Craig when he announced one Sunday that it seemed ridiculous for him to spend the hour and a half at church entertaining Lauren in the social hall, which was like a gym with many doors, so it was a very difficult place to keep her safe.

After a year or so of not attending church, I began attending Sunday morning Mass with Bryn. I was there as a good example for my daughter, but in my heart I was bitter. Sitting amidst complete families was difficult. I remember one Sunday watching a baby explore her father's face as he quietly smiled and whispered to her. I sat watching with tears streaming down my face. I remembered Bryn doing that same thing to her dad in Mass, grabbing his glasses off his face. Lauren was four years old at the time and had never shown any interest in anyone's face or glasses. Hearing simple sermons about loving your neighbor, and starting by serving your family, was frustrating. With a child who rarely slept, I was in servitude to my family twenty-four hours a day in a way that the rest of this congregation would probably never know.

One Sunday, I attended the evening Mass, which was supposed to be geared toward teens. The music was more contemporary and there was a full band with percussion, electric, bass and rhythm guitars. After attending this Mass a few weeks, I decided that I would love to be a part of this group. I had been a guitarist and vocalist in a church folk group for a few years as a teen, and I had been a soprano in my high school choir. When I spoke to Patty, the band leader, she said that, in fact, they were in need of a soprano. I attended the group's next practice and became part of the band. Over the years since that day, these people have become some of my best friends.

Having a reason to sing God's praises (because I have committed to do so) has done much more for my faith than worshiping in community without that obligation. Even on days when I'm so angry at God that I don't personally feel the words I'm singing, I sing because I've made a commitment to the group. Just as faking a smile can turn your heart happy, so can singing God's praises make you desire to praise Him.

I still sit through Masses where the priest talks about knowing God's love by serving others and I can't stop thinking, "I'll provide you that opportunity. Come to my house and babysit for twenty-four hours. Then, let's talk." I know there are other ways to serve and other people who may be as needy as my daughter, but I can't think of any who are as difficult to serve as my daughter. I often sit in church fantasizing about having the opportunity to experience other ministries. When the children were babies, Craig and I looked forward to one day participating as a family in Habitat for Humanity, the ministry that builds homes for those who would probably otherwise never have one. However, Lauren won't be on a work site any time soon. I have recently had a heart for prison ministry, but I don't think Craig will sign on to extra "parenting alone" time while I pursue the soul of an inmate.

Craig and I have discussed and accepted that raising this family is our first and foremost ministry and it leaves little time for any other. We support other favorite ministries as best we can both financially and in prayer. I used to be in charge of fundraising for a large Christian nonprofit organization. Some days, arranging the needs of this one family seems to require as much ingenuity and resourcefulness as pulling off a huge fundraising event.

Craig and I talked often about his desire to go to church and how wrong it was that there was no "place" for Lauren in our church. When we dropped Bryn off at the church for her Sunday School classes, Lauren would often become upset and gesture for us to let her out of her seatbelt as well. She saw all the children walking into the church school building, then playing as they waited for their parents to pick them up afterward. Lauren understandably wanted to be a part of this apparent fun. One day, as she whined and roughly gestured for me to undo her seatbelt, I leaned into the back seat and said, "You can't go in there, Sweetie." At that moment, I saw a little girl pass by Lauren's window. How ridiculous I must sound, I thought, telling her there's no place for her here, when there's obviously a place for all these other little girls her age and size.

During the summer when Lauren was seven, I was suddenly inspired, and surprisingly feeling energetic enough to follow through on my inspiration. I had spoken to our pastor two years earlier about a desire to start some kind of program for families who had a difficult time attending church because of a child's special needs. When a notice in the bulletin brought forth no other families, the pastor said to me, "Well, I guess there isn't a need here right now." I don't know why I didn't jump up and down in front of him and say, "Oh, yes! I'm stand-ing right here in front of you!" Instead, I agreed and didn't bring it up again for two years. I guess the sadness and injustice of feeling like Lau-ren wasn't welcome in our house of worship worked within me over those two years. Craig and I had gotten into the habit of speaking cyn-ically about our church in private. He saw the church body's lack of reaching out to us at a time when we had many great needs as a kind of hypocrisy. I knew we were headed toward having to make a choice. We needed either to leave this church, or to make something happen within the church. When I wrote the following letter to the priests of our church, I guess I was letting their reaction make the decision for us. After some introductions in the letter, I wrote:

I am writing about the need for ministry to a homebound population: Chil-dren with disabilities that prevent them from attending traditional Mass or PSR[29], and their families. But don't panic, as I believe I can play a big part in responding to this need.

Five years ago, the younger of my two daughters, Lauren, was diagnosed with autism. Within the year that followed, our family's involvement at [the church] declined, as it became impossible to attend Mass as a family. Lau-ren is virtually non-verbal and has many sensory issues that prevent her from staying in a pew for more than a few minutes without making a huge disturbance.

About two years ago, I approached [the pastor] with a desire to arrange some kind of child care at the church for Lauren during Mass, so that she could at least become acquainted with the building and people and might someday be able to join us for at least part of Mass, if not all of it. (She learns, grows and changes every day, so I don't give up hope of that.) [Father] was very sympathetic and wanted to help any others with the same need, so we posted a request on the bulletin board and in the bulletin for other parents to call me. When there was no response, [Father] under-standably concluded that the need didn't exist outside my own family and I let the idea fizzle.

Unfortunately, the fact that this population is homebound makes the prob-lem a hidden one. They are not going to be in a place where such an ad is posted. But the problem is pervasive. Permit me to tell you more about *myself, that you might understand why my insights on the problem are valid.*

For the local Autism Society of America chapter, I have been board member, newsletter editor and secretary, which put me in the position of first contact for many parents, teachers (and even one Sunday School teacher) who want to talk. I am a trained parent contact for [a parent support organization], which connects parents with other parents of children with similar disabilities. I spent a year teaching in a program for children with special needs. I have worked as Communications Manager for a[n]...organization...that served hundreds of adults with disabilities every year. I also have waited for years, and continue to wait, in waiting rooms talking to parents of other children with disabilities while Lauren is in therapy. When speaking with people with disabilities or their parents about such topics as "Why me?" it's hard not to bring up Christianity, particularly with another Christian. I have spoken to many parents specifically about church. I hope you agree that this experience qualifies me to speak for other families in our community. (I also hope that it qualifies me to offer and help bring about a solution.)

My own family's experience is much like many other families' with whom I have spoken. When Lauren was diagnosed, we were offered no help in any form from our church. When she became old enough to attend PSR, no alternatives were offered to us, though our situation was well known to many involved. When Lauren's behavior made it impossible to keep her in church with us, our obvious and best option was to discontinue going to Mass. For a while, Craig and I attended different Masses, one of us taking our older daughter, Bryn. But that soon ended, as the sacrifice of two more hours per week without Dad's help was too much for me. Craig had enthusiastically joined our church after completing the [required] program in 1993, five months before Lauren was diagnosed. He now has no church experience, though he longs for it. I originally joined the band partly as motivation to attend Mass with Bryn on Sunday. With this special group of people around me and the extra purpose of attending, I'm able to fight the visions of our little family sitting down front all together. That had been my vision since sitting directly in front of the altar with my family every Sunday and holy day as a child, so it's hard to understand God's plan for our family.

The need for families to attend Mass together is not the only problem. Developmentally disabled children also have spiritual needs. They have questions about God and the universe that, if answered incorrectly, may lead them onto dangerous paths. Because their value is often questioned by the abortion/euthanasia-happy secular world, these children need constant reassurance that they're cherished by God and should be cherished by man. They need exposure to God's Word. They need teaching and examples of how to live a Christian life. (Particularly as it will help them understand that people who treat them cruelly are NOT examples of Christ's love.) At the least, disabled children should not be made to feel that church is a place where brother and sister are welcome, but they are not.

I once spoke to the mother of a child with autism who, though raised Catholic, was attending a Protestant church an hour and a half away from her home because it had Sunday programs for people of all ages with disabilities. I thought it was so sad that the response of her Catholic parish was such that she needed to drive three hours on Sunday to find a spiritual home. I also lauded her for prioritizing her faith and giving up all that time on the weekend to fulfill her spiritual needs and obligations. I also thought, "If you build it, they will come." That church so far away had built it and they came from far and wide.

My husband, Craig, and I have recently considered looking elsewhere for a church that would be open to allowing our family to attend as a family. However, we have both been active at [this church], and we love the priests and the people here. We don't want to consider giving up the Eucharist, any Sacrament or our tradition. We want our home church to be our home.

The fact remains that Lauren cannot attend church at this time, but I am willing to begin a program appropriate for her during Mass. I hope you will discuss this at whatever meeting is necessary for making such a mission happen. I am willing to come at any point to answer questions about the logistics. Here are some answers to some questions you or someone else may have right away.

In the next part of the letter, I addressed some specific logistical questions to provide the priests with a visual picture of this program fitting in well with the existing programs. I also mentioned a timeline (as finding teachers would probably take time) and I offered to direct every aspect of this adventure, which took most of the responsibility out of their laps. I ended with:

Thank you so much for your time. I look forward to hearing more about bringing this ministry to life.

I have reprinted this letter here almost in its entirety not to impress you with my ability to convince, or to sway your opinion of any church. I reprint it because I have wondered if someone else might benefit from it. Another mom or dad who reads this book may have given up hope of their child ever setting foot in a church again. If any of these words may be helpful in convincing you, a pastor, church elder, or rabbi of the importance of doing everything possible to welcome and include people with developmental disabilities, then they need to be here. If you want to use any part of this letter to pursue your own family's needs within your church, feel free to call these words your own.

About a week after I hand-delivered these letters, I received a phone call from the church pastor. He told me three times that the letter was beautiful, and added the important part somewhere in between: "We'll do it."

There was another mother of a child with autism who responded this time to announcements about the Special Needs PSR class. Before classes began, however, she decided that having her son attend this class would be one more obligation than she could handle, even if it would allow her to go to Mass. When Lauren walked into her Sunday School class for the first time, she was the only student and there were two volunteer teachers.

Before the first class, I gave the two teachers a crash course on autism, how it affects Lauren and the care she requires. One of the women was a full-time special education teacher of teenagers with autism. She was polite as I went over information that she probably could have expressed at least as well as I. By the end of the school year, this teacher was familiar with Lauren's specific needs, and she was giving me invaluable advice on dealing with the school system to create a program to meet these needs. Both women became two of Lauren's, and her family's, favorite people.

Since this Sunday School class began, we've had some teacher transitions. First, one of the original teachers left to move to another state.

Then the second teacher left because a new home business was taking up all her free time with her husband. We're currently on our third Sunday School teacher, another patient lady whom Lauren usually enjoys going to the classroom to see while Mom, Dad and Bryn are in church. Another transition may take place soon. Lauren is sometimes upset about having to go to the classroom and asks to stay home or to stay in the car. She's currently on hiatus for the summer, which will give us a few months to decide on the next appropriate step in our family's church needs. (Regular Sunday School classes at our church are in recess every summer.)

Craig and I are always wondering about the best timing for trying to take Lauren into church during Mass with us. Just like toilet training and any skill we introduce to her, this will take time, a plan, commitment, consistency and flexibility. The real question is not whether Lauren is ready. It's whether Craig and I are ready. It's going to be difficult. We may miss many parts of Mass. We'll probably get the evil eye from some people who won't understand the greater good of making room for this person who is a baptized member of their community.

Craig and I also talk about what God expects from His people. Are we failing to live out His commandments if we don't worship in community because it's just too difficult? Is an at-home daily Bible reading and prayer time adequate for a family who was given, by God, this blessing of a child who cannot sit through any portion of a church service? Being raised Catholic, I also have to face the question of the necessity of receiving the Eucharist and some other traditional obligations of my faith. Let's see, if Lauren is beating up on Craig or herself, Craig is understandably very discouraged, and the last scheduled Mass for the weekend starts in five minutes, do I say, "Sorry, Craig, I have an obligation to God to fulfill. You're on your own," and walk out the door? I sincerely believe that Craig and I are in step with God's will when we feel led to live out our Christianity by serving each other at home, rather than by going to church.

I also believe that my spirituality has very little to do with my ability to participate in any organized church gathering. The moments I have seen the face of God have consistently been in situations when I have been serving (or struggling with) a person in need. When I am completely empty and at my greatest moments of despair, I have to turn to God, as there is no other. Craig is supportive, but he has the same despair to overcome and we're both only human creatures. I've heard people say, "We lean on each other" to express how one person in a relationship supports the other when he or she is in need. In Craig's and my case, we would both fall over if we had only each other to lean on!

In the early days after Lauren's diagnosis, usually when Craig was "down" I was "up" and vice versa. We could often pull each other out of an emotional rut. Lately, as some of the problems we've had to face have grown, this nice little give-and-take isn't always there. When one of us is down, it's usually for a reason that seems like an insurmountable problem to both of us. When neither of us has any answers or enthusiasm left, that's when the Holy Spirit steps in. That's when an answer neither of us had seen before whispers itself into one of our ears. We become re-inspired to take up the fight and refreshed by the gentle reminder of who is truly in control and where our hope ultimately lies. This is spirituality at its finest. It resides not in places designated holy, but is called forth by the daily churning and grinding of doing God's will. It reveals itself in the revived and changed heart of a man or woman. It also reveals itself in the smile of a grateful child.

This is what I mean when I say that autism has affected our family the most spiritually. We sing a song at church called "I Want to Know You." Its refrain goes:

> *I want to know You*
> *I want to hear Your voice*
> *I want to know You more*

I want to touch You
I want to see Your face
I want to know You more[30]

I'm learning, while at my daily grind, that if I want to know God better, I should look closely into the faces of my children and my husband. I've seen Him in the face of my husband while he was holding Lauren down at the doctor's office for some procedure or another, sweat dripping off his brow revealing the strength required. I knew his gentle, reassuring words (barely heard over Lauren's screams) were meant to comfort and reassure me, as well as Lauren. This man's dedication to carrying his family smoothly past the painful moments is sometimes a tangible source of strength that makes me buck up, just so he'll realize what a fine job he's doing.

I've heard God's voice somewhere mixed in with a very young Bryn's, when we were talking about what improvement we'd seen in her sister. "I like that Lauren is doing some more things," she shared, "but I hope she never talks too much because then...well, then she wouldn't be Lauren. I just don't like thinking about that."

I've felt the presence of God in the countless times that I've reached out for a hug from Lauren and she's slowly backed into my arms like a delivery truck into a parking space. Her head is always down and her hands shield her eyes, but there's usually a little smile on her lips. She's probably fighting internal explosions of anxiety every time, just to give me what I need—reassurance that she knows how much I love her.

And I've known God was standing right there in the room with us when my husband watched one of these hugs take place and, without a word from me, said, "She knows, Honey. She knows."

PART III
Little Ditties

o o o o o o o o o o o o o o o o o o o o o o o o o o o o o o o o

Ring the bells that still can ring,
Forget your perfect offering.
There's a crack in everything...
That's how the light gets in.

——*Leonard Cohen*

A Child First

The earlier the diagnosis, the better. If you're the parent of a child with autism, you have probably heard that phrase at least once since receiving your child's diagnosis. And it's certainly true. I'm grateful that my daughter, Lauren, was diagnosed as young as nineteen months old. However, believe it or not, there's a negative side to receiving a diagnosis, and a label, so early.

At nineteen months old, Lauren was a beautiful, very quiet, perfectly behaved toddler. (So we were overly blessed with friends and relatives who dismissed our months of searching for answers and said things like, "Oh, she'll talk soon enough. Stop looking for trouble where there is none.") Upon receiving the diagnosis, however, my husband and I suddenly had a difficult time focusing in on Lauren's beauty and peacefulness. We now looked at her and saw a set of symptoms. Whereas we used to think that her steady back-and-forth step to some music from a children's video was adorable, we now saw her dancing and thought, "Oh, no...see, she is autistic," even though her older sister, Bryn, has swayed to music since infancy.

When Lauren was about fourteen months old, I was sitting in the middle of a crowded pew in our church with Bryn and Lauren, who was on my lap facing outward. My husband was sitting in the front pew with a group of people for a special part of the service. A quiet and solemn moment had just begun...and so did a fit of laughter on my lap. My husband was the only person in front of me who didn't turn around, because he knew exactly from where the laughter was coming. I knew he was smiling, and despite my wasted efforts to hush my baby, so was I. The people around me must have thought someone was quite inappropriately encouraging or tickling the child, so I was a little embarrassed. But Craig and I were mostly delighting in this beautiful laughter, because this was one of only very few times we had heard it, or Lauren's voice.

A few months later, a pediatric neurologist asked me if my daughter ever laughed uncontrollably for long periods of time. In that second, this cherished sound became a symptom instead of a joy.

When Lauren was twenty-six months old, she threw a tantrum (for a legitimate reason our detective selves later realized.) With my older daughter, I had always handled such situations as natural occurrences and never became overly upset by them. But this one made me very upset. This seemed to be a new aspect of Lauren's autism that took me off guard. I wondered if I would be able to handle what the future would bring. We went to the pediatric neurologist for a regular visit, and we told him. "That's great!" he said. "Do you realize she's acting like any normal two-year-old? What did she do when she used to be upset? She shut down. Now she's choosing to act outwardly—to communicate to you that she's ticked off! That is so wonderful!" I see my friends' two-year-olds throwing tantrums all the time and tell them not to worry about it; it's often part of being two. But it took a pediatric neurologist to tell me to allow my child to be two.

A few months ago, I heard Lauren making some musical sounds as she was walking around the house, and I told a visiting friend about auditory stim and methods I had read about to cut it down. I remembered this incident yesterday when I heard my older daughter singing to herself. The song she was singing was not only recognizable, but in tune. I know this wasn't the case when she was two, yet she sang all the time back then. Had I ever called her singing auditory stim?

When Lauren was first diagnosed, Craig and I had her in a program for children with autism for a very short time. She was always happy and willing to be near others when in a comfortable situation, whether a new or an old one. But at this school, she continuously cried and curled up into an inconsolable, unreachable little girl.[31] Even favorite toys from home did not affect her. (This was before I became knowledgeable about her many extreme sensory needs which probably made the environment somehow painful to her.) After about eight days of attendance, a teacher met with me and said that because Lauren was not settling in as quickly as expected, they were working on methods to bring her around. The head teacher had observed that Lauren seemed like a different child when she was in my arms—she was very affectionate and happy with me. They wanted to utilize this pleasant association with Mommy. The teacher asked if I wore any perfume or shampoo that had a scent she would associate with Mommy. They wanted to scent a blanket or scarf with a Mommy smell then reward her with it when she did something positive. For example, if she made a move in the direction of the other children instead of away from them, she would be given the Mommy item. "Then what would happen?" I asked. She said they would give her a minute with the item, then take it away until she did the positive behavior again.

I would never put my older daughter in a daycare that utilized a method I would call "Mommy's love is conditional" so why would I accept it for Lauren? Craig and I decided before the next school day that our twenty-month-old was *first* our baby who needed Mommy full-time, and, maybe second, a little girl with autism. She never attended the school again and we have never regretted our decision.

In an attempt to be as considerate as possible with my words, I use the phrase "child with autism" instead of "autistic child" as often as possible. It makes the *child* more prominent in a sentence than his or her set of symptoms.[32] But being considerate with my words doesn't mean much if belief and action aren't behind it. I'm a good parent who believes both of my children are whole, spectacular persons. Yet in practice, I catch myself viewing them through the array of labels the world places on them, as well as my personal feelings about these labels. I'm trying not to do so, in every small way each day.

Our daughters get baths every evening. Some evenings, it's not very convenient, such as when we're out very late and they are almost asleep when we get home. In such a case, Bryn will sometimes forego a bath until the next morning. When Craig suggests that Lauren is too tired for one, too, I insist that we remain in routine, because I know that routine is important to most people with autism. Craig sighs as we force a very tired and unhappy toddler into the tub. In honor of recognizing her as a child first, I think I might let Lauren go to bed dirty the next time we stay out late. Bryn has survived it numerous times, maybe Lauren would, too.

Decorating with Autism

When I was growing up, my parents decorated their house in the Early American style. When I married, my parents and in-laws generously handed down some older pieces of furniture, allowing my husband and me our own style, which we endearingly called Early Attic. Sometime during the last three years, however, we've renamed our decorating style to reflect its strongest influence. We now decorate in Early Autism.

For those unfamiliar with the Early Autism style, the name doesn't reflect choices of furniture and accessories as much as their placement. (Though this style probably does preclude glass-topped tables and any elaborate display of interesting knick-knacks.) It's not a style purposely chosen. Rather, it's one gradually grown into, usually unwittingly.

For us, the transition likely began the day we sent our end tables to the attic. Our two-year-old daughter with autism loved to sit on these tables. At first, this was no great concern as they were sturdy hard-rock maple still virtually smooth and shiny after over twenty years of abuse from uncoastered drinks, as well as children. But when our little girl's seating choice became an issue of contention at the houses of friends (who put silly things on their end tables like lamps and crystal dishes) we decided we had to address our child's preference as inappropriate behavior.

After many days of frustration and anger, I remember throwing myself on the sofa in surrender, when I saw it. As I looked at my daughter sitting on an end table, I finally saw that end table as she did—it looked like a chair! It was a large platform on four legs with a smaller raised platform at the back. It was placed in a room full of chairs no less, and it was more her size than any of the others. At that moment, I cheered up instantly, told my little one how very smart she was, then phoned my husband to tell him the end tables were leaving that evening.

Actually, I now remember that it was the day the ceramic lamps went to the attic that our decorating transition began. The lamps once sat on those end tables, but they were in the way when the tables were used as chairs. (Thank God for overhead lighting.)

One day, I was wasting time mourning my limitations in decorating when a silly "what if" thought turned my mood around. I imagined that I had won a free home makeover by some famed decorator. This person, whom I'll name Martha Stewart, for lack of a better name, would come into my home with the intention of helping me make my world more comfortable, stylish and attractive.

My tour with Martha begins in the living room, where she immediately comments on the placement of the sofa in the middle of the room. "How about pushing it up against the picture window? It would really open up the space." I tell her that's not possible because it gives my daughter a stepping stool to the window sill, and there's nothing she would rather do than stand in the window all day.

"OK," says Martha, "then how about against this great big wall here?" I tell her that's also not a good idea, as the wall makes as great a seat back as the sofa, and we could forget about hanging pictures within reach of little hands. (I haven't decided whether I would tell Martha I have a child with autism. She's so gracious, it may be more fun to let her quietly believe I'm just a parent with a severe discipline problem.)

Martha sighs, moves into the hallway and stops. "May I ask why there are bolt locks on the outsides of all these doors," she nervously asks.

"Well, behind door number one is my bedroom," I offer, "which also houses the cats' litter box ever since someone discovered it made a terrific sandbox, too. Behind door number two is the bathroom, which includes a toilet, of course. When the *No Swimming* sign failed to deter one family member, this lock was installed. Behind door number three is simply a storage closet where I keep laundry hampers. Trust me, if this door were unlocked there would be dirty clothes all over the house and a laundry hamper teetering on the edge of the dining room table with a gleeful little girl inside of it."

Martha slowly nods and doesn't ask me to unlock the doors. We move into the dining room. "That's an interesting flat plate light fixture on the ceiling," she says, "but I would recommend a simple chandelier to add a little warmth."

"Oh, there was a chandelier here when we moved in and it did look nice over the table," I agree. "But that particular chandelier didn't hold up very well to being spun. The day it dropped two feet from the ceiling was memorably frightening for us all. I don't think we'll have another one any time soon."

Martha looks at the ceiling as though it's possessed, shakes, resumes her composure then notices the antique dresser against the wall. "What a lovely piece," she comments. "The runner and basket dress it up nicely, but it's a little barren."

"How about this?" I offer, as I open a drawer and pull out a pair of candles in decorative holders and place them on each side of the basket.

"Perfect!" Martha smiles. Then my children run in, one little girl being chased by another. The smaller one suddenly stops at the dresser, takes a candle by its holder in each hand and continues on her way.

"She collects pairs," I tell an amazed Martha.

We move through the house in a similar fashion and finally end up in the kitchen. "I noticed that the microwave is in the dining room," Martha observes. "This space next to the refrigerator seems to be just right for that."

"Yes, it is," I reply. "But do you see that ceiling fan? My daughter can scale the microwave cart and refrigerator in an instant in order to spin that fan. So we leave that space empty for safety's sake."

Martha nods her head in instant acceptance. Though we haven't made any decor changes, Martha smiles and says, "I believe I'm finished here." To my look of confusion, she adds, "You decorate in a unique style that's comforting and considerate of people's needs. I especially liked the bouncing motif, which I've never seen before, created by the spring horses and trampolines throughout. I also marvel at the use of comforters, pillows and stuffed animals to create cozy nooks in corners. I wouldn't change a thing!"

Sharing Perspective

I n my state, there is an organization called Parent to Parent, for which I am a referral parent. Parents or family members of a person with a disability may call in to request information about various disabilities and available local services. They may also ask to be connected with another parent of a child with the same disability. The majority of calls are from parents of young children with new diagnoses. Parent To Parent keeps its records of referral parents up-to-date so they may match, as closely as possible, the inquiring parent to a family who has experience in the area in which they're interested. For example, I've received a few calls from parents who are interested in homeschooling their child with autism because I'm listed as a homeschooling mother in the organization's files.

I met my first mom of a child with autism through Parent To Parent. I received a call from Teri a few days after my call for help to Parent To Parent. There happened to be an autism support group meeting that evening and Teri called me to ask if I would like to come. I met her at a convenient location, where she also picked up another mom of a son with a recent diagnosis. Teri drove us the rest of the way to a church building where we encountered a whole new world of people and information. After the meeting, we three women (and one other mom) stood in the parking lot outside the church, laughing, telling stories and sharing ideas until after midnight. Teri felt like a dear friend by the time I got back into my car to drive home. She's been a source of information, empathy and laughter, ever since.

Teri is the ultimate parent for helping parents with a new diagnosis. Her daughter is nine years older than Lauren, and has always been less developmentally delayed than Lauren. Teri was working on getting her daughter into a regular public school classroom back when autism wasn't a recognized diagnosis in our state's special education program. Despite the differences in our children and our autism experience, the moment I started speaking to her on the phone, Teri obviously understood everything I was rambling on to her about my daughter, my feelings and my, as yet uneducated, "mom's intuition." She understood that I saw in my baby girl what no doctor had seemed to see behind their official declarations and recommendations. She encouraged me to follow my gut instincts and to become the expert on my child.

Teri has been in and out of many organizations, school situations and political advocacy groups over the years, but has never stopped taking calls from parents of young children with a new diagnosis. A few months ago, I was complaining to her that I sometimes dread calling the person whose name and phone number I have just received from Parent To Parent. (I worry that my being in a very different place from these people will prevent me from making a connection. This leads me to wonder if someone closer to their situation might be a better contact.) Teri reminded me of how we first met and reassured me that whatever I had to say was beneficial.

Probably one reason I don't like to talk to new parents is my consternation at the advanced knowledge they seem to have for newcomers. When a mom tells me her child speaks about twenty words and is already on a gluten-free diet, I realize that it's only moments before she realizes I'm not much of a mentor. I eventually have to respond that my daughter still has no consistently usable language and that our family also just began the gluten-free diet. When she starts to advise me on the best places to find gluten-free products, I consider hanging up on the little whipper snapper! I've never hung up, though (as it takes me a minute to find a pencil to jot down the name of the store she recommends) and after about twenty minutes, I'm glad I didn't.

Information is much more readily available for parents of autistic children than it was even when Lauren was diagnosed. In the early years after Lauren's diagnosis, I received many articles about autism from friends and family who wanted to help. Most were biographies of families dealing with autism, and the point of the article was usually to portray, as realistically as possible, the family's legitimate sense of hopelessness. (I don't know if I ever officially stopped saying "Thank you" when handed one of these, or if it just naturally turned into, "Yep, read it already!") There were two or three prevailing educational theories at the time, each having its own miracle poster child, but there was no evidence that any of these successes could be duplicated in a child with a firm autism diagnosis.[33]

Within the last few years, the amount of television reporting on autism, celebrity attention to autism and magazine coverage of autism has exploded. This is primarily because of recent discoveries of successful and duplicable dietary and physiological interventions, such as gluten- and casein-free diets and secretin. Today, newcomers to autism may be encouraged by health professionals to find hope in widely available documented statistics. Less than a decade ago, hope was more likely to be discouraged by professionals, but held privately by parents despite statistics.

Though hope supported by statistics is great to have after being so long without it, it's not what parent-to-parent support is all about. When I get past the initial information exchange (which tends to be all my new parent friends are looking for at the start of a phone call) the important stuff begins. That's when I get to be more to this person than another multi-media information source—as attractive and interactive as I am in that role. That's when it hits—the reality of finding and speaking to another human being on this earth who understands the grief of mothering a beloved child in the harshest of conditions. This person understands the pain, the anger, the spiritual challenge, the physical challenge, the grief over *everything* that is lost. She also understands the spurts of wisdom and intense joy that are unexpected blessings in the unlikeliest of places when you love a child with autism. Friends and relatives often don't grasp that last one. That's something only parents of a child with autism (or another extreme diagnosis) can confidently nod about.

Conversation with a new mom friend often takes a delightful turn when she tells me where her child is developmentally. (I talk about moms instead of parents because I've only provided support phone calls to women so far.) Compared to Lauren's capabilities at her child's age, or even now, her child usually sounds very capable, so I say, "That's great!" It's not empty encouragement. I've taught enough, met enough and read enough about children with autism that I know the potentialities of a child who is talking in short, complete sentences at three years old, or who is toilet-trained and eats a healthy diet of fruits and vegetables at four. These are important indicators of the depth of his or her problems.

Prior to our conversation, the mom has usually encountered only medical doctors who have presented a discouraging picture of her child's future. Medical doctors speak in terms of deficiencies. A medical diagnosis is an assessment of what's wrong with a person, not what's right. When this mom describes her child as a list of symptoms and I say, "That's great!" this may be the first time anyone has been positive about her son or daughter since the diagnosis. My positive reaction usually leads to my new friend bravely sharing some other positive things she's noticed or long held dear about her child, and our relationship is off and running. (After this conversation, we may never speak to each other again, as she'll find people who are closer sources of strength, but our short-lived relationship will have served an important purpose.)

Parents with a new diagnosis, or even an old diagnosis, often step back from their children so they can see them as the professionals do, assessing their needs, developing strategies, choosing programs, then trying to make those programs work. Professionals, friends and relatives often expect them to perform these tasks without a thought about the emotional strain, not because they're insensitive, but because it's necessary. It's Mom and Dad who know the child best and want the best for them, so they make the best advocates. So what a joy, on occasion, to inquire about a mom or dad's thoughts and feelings and to honor their heart and their instincts by affirming them. Some people can do this only by listening, and by trusting that what this parent shares is true, never questioning it. Another mom or dad who's been there can actually say "Amen to that!" and raise them one by sharing a similar story or observation. The opportunity I have to do this for so many people is a gift, particularly as they usually return the favor within the same conversation.

I was once trying to convey to a mom with a new diagnosis that her son was the same sweet little guy that he was the day before he received the label of PDD/Autism. She told me that the doctor had said that this was a lifelong condition and that it would change their lives drastically. He suggested that her boy had no future and blatantly declared this diagnosis to be the worst possible in the field of pediatric neurology. I explained to her that this man was a medical doctor, that his job requires him to look at the deficits to provide a diagnosis, but in this case, his diagnosis was wrong. (I was even shocked with myself when I said this, but I knew where I was going, and I had a few years of experience with a child with many more challenges than her son, so I was confident.)

"Autism is a medical condition with physical symptoms, right?" I continued quickly.

"Right…" the woman hesitantly followed.

"Think of another medical condition for which you would go to a doctor with a group of symptoms, for example, a headache."

"O.K." she agreed.

"What is the worst kind of headache you can imagine? There are tension headaches. There are migraines…"

"Oh, they're terrible," she said.

"Yes, but have you ever known someone who went to the doctor because of a severe headache and it turned out to be a brain tumor?" I asked.

"Uh, no…"

"Well, I have," I said. "Some of the symptoms are the same as with a migraine. Severe headache, nausea, sometimes dizziness and loss of vision. A migraine is not fatal, but a brain tumor is often fatal or terribly detrimental to the person's future." I took a breath and asked, "If your son had this cluster of symptoms, which diagnosis would you hope he had, a migraine or a tumor?"

"A migraine, of course!"

I spoke quickly as I was afraid she'd hang up on me at the ridiculousness of the question, "Well, your son was misdiagnosed. He has a migraine, not a brain tumor." Silence. "I get migraines," I explained. "They're horrible. My doctor treats them very seriously, they greatly impact the quality of my life and I often need my family's help to get past a bad episode. There are a lot of things doctors have learned recently that help many people with migraines. Physiologically, there are medications from Tylenol to prescription drugs that might help. Diet changes and nutritional supplements can also make a big difference." (I was beginning to see the huge correlation between migraines and autism.) "When I feel a migraine coming on, I help myself by modifying the environment. I lie down on a soft surface in a quiet and dark room. Long term, I try to keep my schedule and my surroundings as simplified and uncluttered as possible since I know chaos contributes to my stress and migraines always follow a period of stress."

My new friend was still quiet, so I hoped for the best and finished my analogy. "Autism is really, really bad, but it's not the worst diagnosis you could get. It will sometimes make your life miserable, but there are physiological interventions, nutritional interventions, educational interventions and environmental accommodations you can make…"

"It sounds a lot like a migraine."

"Only worse," I admitted.

"But not a brain tumor," she said.

"Not a brain tumor."

"Thank you so much," she said. "I can't wait to tell that to my husband." Hooray! I hadn't completely blundered as a support person.

"Oh, and in between really bad episodes," I added, "you have your family and you can love them to pieces."

"That doctor was a real idiot," she said.

"Yep," I agreed. After a few more "thank-you's" and "nice-to-talk-to-you's," we hung up and I wandered around my kitchen trying to remember what I was doing before my phone rang, knowing in the back of my brain that I should quickly search for Lauren. But I always walk in circles for a few minutes after a conversation like that, to allow it time to settle into my brain so I'm sure not to lose it, I guess. When I was finally ready to push open some doors and look for Lauren, I felt the smile on my face as I actually said aloud, "I'm so glad I get migraines."

"I'm sick, Mom"

In the late summer twilight, your delicate profile is gently illuminated by the glow of the picture window. As you gaze at the television, your reliable bedtime video comforts you for the moment. Wisps of hair, only wet at the tips now, an hour after your bath, bend in front of your ear and fan out toward your face, directing attention to your delicate gray-green eyes, barely colorful under the glow of the room's dimmed light. The slope of your nose is a gentle line rounding out at a perfect distance to form the tip of your nose. So rarely do I have the opportunity to just look at you from this angle. Your pale lips are full and soft in this serene instant. If I possessed the perspective of this moment only, I might envy the physical gifts God has bestowed on you.

My perspective changes as you draw your lips back tightly and squeeze your eyes shut. A moan ever so slowly makes its way from deep within you, turning slowly into the high-pitched sob that fills my ears and my heart. You draw your hands to your eyes and press two fingers to each lid. The warmth of tears on your cheeks seems to alarm you, as it always does, they come so rarely. In between batting and rubbing them with your fingers, your eyes grow wide as you try to stop the flow. You turn to me in confusion about the whole matter, slowly letting out a deeply drawn breath that turns into another wail, then another, then another.

Thankfully, we have a double-wide upholstered chair. You normally don't let me sit next to you for long, but tonight, I rub your leg in rhythm with my attempts at reassurance. I catch myself lying every now and then, saying, "It's OK." Or "You're OK." Then I realize that I have no idea whether you're OK. In fact, you have been sobbing most of the last hour, so you're probably not OK. "You'll feel better, Lauren." I change my mantra. "I promise this yucky feeling will go away, and hopefully, it will go away soon. Let's pray to make it go away." And I speak a prayer aloud, directly to Jesus, from both of us.

I have no idea what yucky feeling I'm talking about. You've been sick with a head cold for over a week, but it seemed to be going away. I presume you had a fever, headache and horrible sore throat with it, as those were my symptoms when I came down with it the same day. Today, I have gobs of congestion in my throat, often making it impossible to swallow. I just attempted to vacuum the car, but I've been dizzy on and off, and bending over to reach the floor mats gave me a sudden headache and wave of nausea. A friend at church this evening told me there was a second wave to the virus I thought we were over. I believe her. Is this what you feel Lauren? Do you have a headache? Are you nauseated? Does your stomach hurt? Can you breathe through your nose and swallow? I know I'll never know the answers to these questions. Not about tonight's illness anyway.

I pray that one day you'll be able to tell me when you hurt. I long to hear, "Mom-m-m-y! I don't feel good!" When I hear Bryn whine these words, I'm not happy to hear them, but I know what to do. I stop what I'm doing. I ask what hurts. I put my hand to her cheek and forehead. I take her complaints seriously and rearrange my schedule. I hug a lot and rub her back. I wrack my brain trying to remember which home remedies and over-the-counter drugs address each symptom best. I would do that for you, too, my Lauren. But instead, too many times I've grown angry at your whining, put you in your room or yelled at you from the front seat of the car, only to have you suddenly throw up. "Ah ha! You're sick!" I thrill at the solving of the mystery, and in the same instant, repent of most of my actions during the last twenty-four hours. If only I'd known, Lauren, I surely would have been more compassionate.

When you're sick, Lauren (which is often the case, thanks to that compromised immune system that came along with the diagnosis), you don't understand why we're putting a bucket in front of you or forcing you to face the toilet. In fact, you've never put up with that smelly nonsense. Why, after all, would any sane person think that looking directly into a mop bucket or commode would make one feel better? If anything, it would make a relatively healthy person take a turn for the worse! Yes, I fully understand your line of reasoning on that one. (But I don't understand how your worst illnesses have been so consistently scheduled with each delivery of new furniture.)

I've read about migraines being a problem for many people with autism, particularly if they have a family history of migraines. I've had migraines that have forced me to lie down on the ground and made me unable to see. My mother and grandmother have a history of these horrific, nauseating headaches, as well. So many times, Lauren, you have lain on your bed, or the floor, or the sofa, moaning, whining or screaming. When I have a bad migraine, your dad comes home from work immediately. I can't imagine not being able to ask for help during the intense pain and illness that accompany it. Are you hurting like this and unable to ask for help, Lauren? Are your whines a cry for help that sends Mom and Dad's nerves up a wall and leads them to act in ways that worsen your pain rather than comfort you?

Gas pains and heartburn can be so intensely painful until relieved. I couldn't begin to count the times that you have thrown a huge fit, Lauren, perhaps hitting someone or hurting yourself in the process, only to be completely over it upon passing gas. That piercing pain in your middle must feel like someone is stabbing you with a long blade. I don't blame you for being so angry with the loved ones around you who aren't fighting to make it stop! It must make no sense when, instead, we fight to make you stop.

Even when we do have a firm diagnosis of a urinary tract infection or ear infection or strep throat, how may I help you, my love? I cherish the memories of nursing my babies to health when they were sick. Whether it was Bryn or you who was sick, we knew it meant lots of rocking, nursing and cuddling. I held you longer before laying you down in bed, gently rubbing your head, pushing your hair back from your face with each stroke. It was probably when you stopped nursing that you also stopped rocking and stopped cuddling. What does that leave us to do when you're sick? I'm an expert at forcing medicine into you through an oral syringe. But afterward, if it was bad-tasting medicine, our relationship is worse off. You're certainly not going to allow me to caress your feverish forehead after I've forced the worst tasting liquid in the world down your throat. (Talk about being kicked when you're down!)

I know your autism makes it hard enough to face the strange day-to-day demands of the people around you. It's hard to look us in the face and to let us hug you when you don't know where our hugs are going or how long they're going to last. But when you're feeling sick and having the toughest time coping, that's all your mom knows to do for you. I want to hug you and caress you, so you can relax and rest, knowing you're loved while you heal. But you tense up and push me away, looking at me with fear and confusion, wondering why, if I love you, I allow this illness to torment you. Oh, my dear Lauren, if ever there were a reason to speak…

A Moment in the Life

I hear her running through the house. She turns into a tornado only when she's naked. Is it the fear or the excitement of getting caught that makes her move so fast?

Six years old and no desire or inclination to sit on the toilet. That's why the stripping is a problem. I really don't mind my child being naked in the privacy of her own home, if it's more comfortable. But I do mind the poop and pee. And so does her dad, who comes home from work to clean multi-room messes, as he knows it's impossible for me to take care of her and clean, too.

Each time I recognize the rhythm of pounding feet, my heart rises into my throat. I look into the family room, but she's turned a corner. I try to catch her head-on in her bedroom (there are two doors) but she must have sensed my plan and doubled back. Or maybe she's now able to become invisible—today it wouldn't surprise me.

Finally, I take the nonchalant approach. My calm step exudes, "No, Mommy hasn't noticed that you're naked, or that you're even near. I'm just fetching something from the dining room." As she curiously sidles up to me, I suddenly seize her hand. She drops to the ground, dead weight, not willing to concede defeat quite yet.

I don't know whether it's because I've just come from five minutes of stolen reading time and am feeling refreshed, or I've subconsciously realized a need for the change, but this time I don't attempt to coax, pull or drag this unwilling body into position to walk to the bathroom. Instead, I squat down, wrap my arms firmly around her and scoop her up as I did when she was a baby—before I knew she had autism—when my foremost thought was always, "Let no harm come to you."

"You must be cold," I say, and she looks up at me in amazement. She senses no frustration about ruined carpeting or hours spent scrubbing floors and washing linens. She senses only unconditional love. With a growing smile, she touches her forehead to mine, looks deeply into my eyes, then quickly licks my lips. We both giggle about our special kiss, then I carry her into the bathroom.

Though I can't promise my reaction to the next stripping episode will be as patient, I hope the memory of this one will help make it so. For though there were no words, I knew what the smile, the touch, the kiss and the giggle were all saying: "You are the coolest mom in the world! I think I *can* be brave again tomorrow—even when things get *really* scary!"

Wisteria

This is the time of year when the wisteria is in full bloom down south. I have a fascination with wisteria. I have a fascination with anything that exudes beauty and ugliness in the same moment. Though the wisteria vine is too thick and its leaves too scarce to provide nice coverage all year, for a few weeks in the spring the flowers are magnificent. And the aroma is inescapable. I know this because wisteria has meandered from my neighbor's back yard over some branches and across some overgrown shrubbery outside my kitchen. For a very short time each year, I walk out my back door and am almost knocked over by the scent and hue surrounding me.

Today I drove down a road lined with a wall of wisteria. From afar, the lavender flowers were attractive, but the delicate perfection of each blossom certainly wouldn't have been apparent to anyone without wisteria experience. The flowers droop from gangly vines with small pale green leaves, so there's no strong contrast. The flower color is pale in comparison to the azaleas, forsythia and hyacinth that bloom in yards everywhere at the same time of year. Wisteria are true wallflowers—likely to go unnoticed by those looking for the obvious bright splashes of color, and by those gazing downward, looking for flowers placed in common fashion in the landscaping.

This year, we're slowly hacking away at the overgrown trees and bushes that support the wisteria outside our kitchen. I'm feeling torn about tearing away at something that requires minimal support to exist. But the original mass in my neighbor's yard will be left to regrow, and the opportunity to reflect on wisteria and the qualities it shares with Lauren has been of value.

This isn't the first dichotomy that has brought Lauren to mind. Craig often refers to our youngest as our "diamond in the rough." Some days, however, there's no denying that she's more like a lion in sheep's clothing!

A few years ago, I was at church and there was a young, enthusiastic missionary priest, named Fr. Brian, saying Mass. He had come from Brazil and had draped the altar with tapestries and blankets woven from the brightest cotton threads I had ever seen. Some had simple silhouettes of farm scenes woven into the design, but most were row after row of color. Hundreds of joyful colors seemed to be used in each piece. Row widths and color choices seemed to be random, as though a free spirit with no thought for order or the difficulties of life had thrown it together in between dances. But looking closely, the taut and meticulous stitches revealed the skill of an experienced craftsman.

Fr. Brian told the congregation that having these pieces around him enabled him to speak easily about his mission, because they exuded the warmth and joy of the people who made them. Then he talked about the living conditions of his friends in Brazil. They have no running water, bathrooms or televisions. Many have lost family members to common illnesses because of the inaccessibility of medical care. They speak of Americans as friends and without jealousy, even though they know what prosperity we live in! Externally, these people would seem pitiable to us Americans. But it wasn't the external Fr. Brian wanted us to see, as he knew that would cloud our minds from the truth. It was the tapestries that best revealed them, and their spirits.

After Mass, I looked over the products that Fr. Brian had brought from his Brazilian friends to sell for the mission. I didn't have enough money to buy a beautiful rug or wall hanging, so I perused the table looking for something inexpensive to take home as a reminder of that night. Fr. Brian walked over to the table and I told him how much his sermon had meant to me because, like his Brazilian friends, my daughter, Lauren, had an amazing and joyful spirit, but her circumstances made it difficult for those using worldly standards to see it. I told him I was looking for something in vibrant colors to remind me of her vibrant spirit when even I was judging her by worldly standards.

Fr. Brian pulled a beautiful blanket out of a pile and said, "Here, this is for Lauren."

"Oh, it's beautiful, but I can't afford that tonight," I said.

"Oh, no, this is for Lauren from Fr. Brian," he clarified. "Tell me more about Lauren, and when I get home, we'll be praying for her, and you can pray for all her friends in Brazil when you see this blanket."

This wasn't a gift to be refused, so I told Fr. Brian about Lauren…and her autism, and some of her challenges, and about her beautiful spirit, and the joy she brings to all those who set aside some worldly standards long enough to glimpse that spirit. Every time I pull that blanket from Lauren's dresser drawer, I think of her friends in Brazil. When she's near, I tell her about their challenges, then point out the bright colors. And I pray that their economic and physical circumstances improve, but that their hearts and their handiwork always remain the same.

Reality

I was driving Lauren home from school, when that feeling in my chest was there—again. I wanted to cry. I wanted to talk to someone. I wanted someone to say, "You go lie down and I'll take care of everything for a while." But I had plans to go to the grocery store, so I tried to put a smile on my face and I spoke to Lauren about her day.

It had been Lauren's first day back to school after Easter weekend. I don't know whether the candy she'd eaten on Sunday was the culprit (it had contained dairy, gluten and artificial ingredients), but Lauren had not done well at school that day. Though her teachers are generally positive, today when I walked into the room, they all looked harried and exhausted. One teacher was standing in a wary stance over Lauren, and when she redirected her, it was not in her usual sing-songy voice. The lead teacher hesitantly told me that Lauren had been pretty happy today, as well as completely out of control. She hadn't joined the group for any activity and hadn't sat down for anything except to eat. She had spent her five hours there running from one piece of mischief to another. I knew exactly what she was describing, as Lauren had been behaving the same way at home over the weekend. I appreciated it (on one level) when the teacher added as I headed out the door, "I feel bad for you, because we have the three of us here tag-teaming and it's hard. I can't imagine having to do that alone for any length of time."

What was upsetting me in the car was not that Lauren had "misbehaved" or disappointed her teachers. It wasn't even that I also had no idea how I was going to handle the next few hours without back-up. (And if you're picturing a S.W.A.T. team when I say "back-up," that's not so ludicrous.) Panic was rising within me because I was at a complete loss. I had no idea what was causing Lauren's difficulties. I had a bunch of theories—gluten she had gotten into on Easter, the weather, a serious yeast overgrowth that I felt guilty about not yet having attacked—but no hard evidence to support any of these theories.

I took Lauren home so she could use the bathroom before going shopping. She struggled and kicked me as I tried to redress her. Normally, I would take physical control of the situation and not tolerate such abuse, but as I grabbed her wrists to protect myself, I saw a wound on the side of Lauren's middle finger. It looked like a large blister had popped and fresh, bright red flesh was seeing the light of day for the first time. My chest muscles tightened and my lungs felt constricted. What had happened to my baby? That's not a place you get a blister from hanging on the monkey bars. Had she burned her finger and no one ever knew? Was she in severe pain, but unable to tell anyone? Did we ignore her or were we even callous to her at the time she was trying to express her pain because she whines so frequently? I knew she wouldn't let me put a cold cloth, antibiotic ointment or a band-aid on it, so I could do nothing to "mother" her at the moment but say "My poor baby" as sincerely as possible.

I could feel my cheeks fill up with a need to cry. I recognized this now for the panic attack that it was. I'd had a few of them since Lauren's diagnosis. My predominant symptom is an overwhelming feeling that I can't handle the responsibility before me. At that moment, I am physically weak—drained—and require every ounce of resolve just to follow through on the simple physical motions of the activity at hand, be it driving, tying a shoelace or dressing my child.

Craig was working at home that day, so I went to his office to speak with him, but he was on the phone. Lauren would be naked again within minutes if I didn't put her in the car, so I had to deal with this myself. I guess God had seen these attacks coming before I did, as about six months before my first one, I had learned that a relative had a history of panic attacks. Though I had never given them any thought before, she had described to me how she talks herself through them. In this instance, I kept telling myself, "We're just going to the grocery store. It's not more than I can handle. I've done it thousands of times before. Lauren will be in her stroller. It's just the grocery store. Focus on the grocery store."

Of course, it wasn't the grocery store that had sent me into a tailspin of self-perceived powerlessness. It was failure. Knowing whether your child is sick or injured is a primary function of being a mother. Being there to ease her pain, or at least sympathize with her during her pain—that's fundamental. I had failed at both tasks and had no idea how to do it any better next time. Usually, when I'm faced with a challenge, I simply find the information I need to decide how to handle it and confidently pursue the solution. But in this instance, as so often with Lauren, there's no information to be had. The source is not speaking and can't even confirm my suspicions. There's nothingness in front of me. I'm free-falling into the future with no footholds. That's a reason to panic.

When I took on the job of mother, it was with the enthusiasm of an astronaut accepting an assignment to Mars. During my maternity leave, I spent a nap-time figuring out how we could afford for me to quit my job, so that I could stay home with Bryn. Craig walked through the door that evening and I announced, "If we sell the car, and live frugally" (I had listed all the numbers) "we can afford to have me stay home." I thought Craig would nervously question the plan initially, so he surprised me when he said, "Great! Let's do it!" Our income immediately dropped to less than half of what we'd been living on. It was very difficult. I was thirty miles from any friends, relatives or shopping, and I had no car. Craig's car was provided by his company.

From time to time in those early years, Craig worked a second job in the evenings. His parents and mine knew we were struggling and helped out at times when they saw a need (for which we are eternally grateful). When arguments began, it was because of stress over money. It was never *about* money, as we both always agreed on our financial plan of action, but *because* of money—it's scary not knowing how you're going to make it until next month. We believe most of our choices have been right for our family. We have consistently agreed upon ideals, then done our best to live according to those ideals.

I often confidently refer to myself as a professional mother. I have read more books about child-rearing, discipline and autism than I ever read for my bachelor's degree, and I have spent years trying to put this information to use for well over forty hours a week, so aren't I a professional in this field? (Congratulations to you if you just realized you were, too.) As a professional mom, I have chosen and developed ideas about the best way to raise a child. Educationally speaking, I was determined to pass on to my daughters a love of literature and a desire to seek information simply to satisfy their own curiosity. I also wanted them to have every opportunity to explore and express their personal creativity.

To fulfill these goals, my plan was four-fold:

1. I would read to them often, at the very least before bedtime.

2. I would have many children's books always available for them within reach.

3. We would visit the library frequently so that they would be comfortable there and familiar with its workings.

4. They would have free access to toys and art supplies, so that they could easily explore and learn about their world in free play and feel comfortable expressing themselves through art.

Now, I wasn't approaching this wearing rose colored lenses. I don't attempt anything without first getting organized. (The words "organization freak" have been applied to me.) Fortunately, we had furniture for only the family room at the time, so when Bryn was a toddler, Craig and I dedicated the living room to the children's development and put plastic storage units all along the walls to neatly keep their toys and art supplies. Bryn has always been obedient and respectful (generally speaking) so she asked before taking down anything complicated and helped when I said it was time to clean up. The system worked beautifully while Lauren was a baby. Even in the early days after her diagnosis, she left virtually everything alone. She was often in her own little world at that time, preferring to stare at her hand rather than to pull paper and markers off a shelf.

When Lauren was about two years old, we decided to pursue the Options Institute method of putting toys up high, so that Lauren would have to initiate some kind of communication to get anything of interest. Suddenly, all of the children's toys were out of reach. Bryn's desk and art supplies were still at ground level, but that didn't last long. Lauren soon learned to use the desk and chair as a stepping stool to a toy she desired, bypassing any need to communicate. She also developed a strong desire to throw things. Though it took only a second to strew all the art supplies across the floor, that second of flinging was worth any discouragement we could conjure, so the art supplies disappeared, too. Bryn's piles of impromptu paintings of Mom or the cats or just a montage of color were a thing of the past. Within a year, even the shelves came down, as Lauren loved to do pull-ups on them and to hear the sound of toys crashing to the floor. I particularly hated the hundreds of dents that a bucket of duplos or matchbox cars could leave on my hardwood floor in seconds. Over the years, the toys have gradually disappeared to the point where closets and toy cabinets have locks on them.

Our beautifully "handcrafted by Grandpa" bookcase of children's books also had to disappear for a few years, as for awhile, there was nothing Lauren enjoyed more than to strew books all over the floor. I tried forcing her to pick them up with me, and even tried turning the bookcase around to face the wall, but she would still find a way to knock the books off the shelves within seconds. Hundreds of thin books took hours some days to pick up. The bookcase finally went into a locked closet. "You'll just have to ask for them when you want some books to read," I told Bryn, and she agreed, understanding the problem.

I proved my educational theories by not implementing them. When Bryn couldn't see her toys or books, she forgot she had them. I hated having the television on, but it often kept Lauren happy, so it was often on and Bryn was in front of it, too. Bryn didn't think to ask for a book or crayons and paper unless I was on top of things enough to suggest it to her. She was always delighted at the idea, but, like most people, Bryn is a visual person. When something isn't visibly available, she's not going to pursue it.

Going to the library became difficult when Lauren started running away from me and having tantrums in public. Though I longingly watched moms and their preschoolers feed the ducks in the pond next to the library, that was also off limits because Lauren didn't understand that there are some bodies of water not intended for swimming. I was grateful that friends could take Bryn to story hour at the library, but I also felt an enormous sense of guilt.

I remember trying to explain my feelings to Craig one day when I was feeling particularly helpless. "Imagine," I said, "that at work, you set out to do what you were hired to do. You research the best way to approach a problem and enthusiastically begin working towards a solution. But at every turn, you're thwarted. Day after day, even though you hate the fact that you're drifting further and further from the best methods to handle this project, you're forced to make compromises. In the end, you complete the project, but no one's very impressed, not even you, because you knew the ideal and you ended up so far from it. Now imagine that this happens on every single project that you undertake. Don't you think you would feel a sense of failure?"

"Yes," he said, "but I could always quit. And my projects are nowhere near as important as your projects."

Hooray! He understood. And now he could begin to understand my overwhelming sense of guilt—these "projects" I'm failing at are the most important in the world.

Feelings of failure and guilt have also arisen from some of my longer term ideals. I've known since I was a teenager that I wanted to get married and have children someday. My formula for success came from my own family, of course, and the priorities I had laid out were simple and reasonable. Two priorities involved church. My family would be at Mass every Sunday, sitting in the front pew so that the children could focus on the priest and the activity at the altar rather than be distracted by misbehaving children in their view. (This was my mother's trick.) And my family would pray before each meal and enjoy conversation at dinnertime.

Lauren has not attended church since she was about two years old. As soon as she discovered that she could crawl under the pews to escape, it became impossible to keep her in the pews with us for even a minute. I attended church with Bryn on and off for a few years without Craig and Lauren, but I felt bitterness burning deep inside of me as I sat there, silently asking God why he would foil a person's plans to attend church as a family. I saw other families sitting together week after week and became angrier. I would think to myself, "You don't appreciate the privilege you're enjoying just being here together." I would critique every word of the priest's homily for an ounce of truth. Unless he was talking about the pain and anguish life on this earth entailed (which our cheery priests never addressed), he wasn't speaking the truth, as far as I was concerned.

Prayer and conversation at dinnertime were just as challenging. For about a year, Lauren didn't want anyone sitting at the table with her, particularly not her sister. She would push us out of our chairs and scream and hit if we refused to budge. Our dinner table had become a battleground. We had the option of letting her eat separately, as we had a child-sized table the girls used for snacks, but I refused to give in on this issue. We began each meal sitting down together, and when Lauren couldn't handle it, she went to her room to calm down. The door was ajar, in case she decided to join us, but this was usually too difficult for her, so we listened to her screaming for most of the meal. I didn't even attempt to pray before eating most meals because I didn't feel thankful at all at that moment.

Though I'll probably never know for sure, I've always believed that Lauren's difficulty at the table was due to the stressful face-to-face interaction required there. Bryn sat directly across from her sister, which helps to explain why Lauren's opposition to her was the most vehement. Lauren also seemed less able to focus directly in front of herself, where her food was, than across the table at someone else's plate. She often seemed angry that Bryn was eating the food on her plate, so I would pull Lauren's plate across the table until she focused on it, show her that she had the same food and push it back to her. I often redirected this way throughout the meal.

Whatever the reason, one day, Lauren was suddenly able to sit at the table with us. But she still became upset easily. I created a rule that dinnertime was to be quiet and calm. We spoke very little, and when conversation became animated or loud, it was put to a halt. Gradually, over the next year, a calm dinner table wasn't necessary for Lauren to stay with us, and in fact, mealtime is now usually Lauren's favorite part of the day. Occasionally, we have to declare a mealtime quiet because Lauren's had a bad day and is very sensitive. But usually, not only is there lively conversation, but Lauren often laughs at some of our jokes and tries to verbalize a story about her own day. When we can make out a word and respond to what she's thinking about, she's tickled down to her toes and giggles along with the rest of us at her success and the joy of sharing in a conversation. Just thinking about this success makes me feel silly writing a chapter about a mom's feelings of failure and subsequent guilt. These special moments can instantaneously make me feel like the most successful person in the whole world.

It's so important to acknowledge a mom's feelings of pain, despondency and failure, but it's even more important that she experiences overriding moments of joy.

Today, we're able to have the children's bookcase out. In fact, it's at the end of Lauren's bed, and I've caught Lauren picking stray books up from the floor in front of it and placing them back on the shelf. Though she won't do this with me, Lauren loves to lie on her or her sister's bed while Bryn sits Indian-style and reads her a picture book with some favorite characters in it. Just having her sister all to herself without an adult dictating the moment seems to tickle her enough to stay until the book's end. Usually, I discover this scene after a panic-stricken race through the house when I realize Lauren's not in one of her usual niches. That's probably why, when I open the bedroom door and find two sisters peacefully enjoying a book (and each other's company), the rush of joy I get supersedes all the anguish, at least for the rest of the day.

Life is still not perfect. There are many weeks that we have our carpet steam cleaner out three or four times to clean up after a BM incident, or a dumped bottle of shampoo, olive oil, detergent or cleaning solution. We call poison control's emergency number at least twice a year (though we haven't been advised to rush to the hospital yet). We have only a few families who still include Lauren in invitations to their homes. Many mornings I wake up to an inexplicably angry child whose whining is like scrap-metal scraping my ears. And Lauren is still at the severest end of the autism spectrum by many criteria.

I think I believed life could be perfect when I entered the jobs of marriage and child rearing. I foresaw heaven on earth in my visions of the family I would have some day. Why not? I'm a talented woman who would only marry a great guy. (I did get that part right.) I knew how to avoid the pitfalls that befall many of America's families and I was confident of the efficacy of my theories on raising children. (All experienced parents, stop chuckling before reading on.) Well, I still believe in the efficacy of my child-rearing theories and some days I wish I had another family to try them on! But for the family God handed me, those theories needed to be thrown out the window (or at least constantly revised until they barely resemble the original ideas). What a lesson in humility.

Today, I'm very aware that life on this earth cannot be perfect. My motivation (when it exists) for waking up in the morning no longer has much to do with the gains and improvements I can make in our lives today. It rarely has to do with foreseeable fun within our plans for the day. I know that what I plan to be a fun activity or outing can turn nightmarish in a heartbeat. But when a fun day *is* had by all, it's never taken for granted and is always appreciated like treasure from Heaven.

My most consistent motivation for getting out of bed each morning is my certainty that this life is but a drop of water in the Niagara Falls of the big picture. I've never been to Niagara Falls (which is a shame, considering I grew up in New York State), but I'm sure the grandeur that awaits me in Heaven will make these falls look like spit in a sink. When I wake up in the morning and realize that Lauren may never talk, I'm able to swing my legs to the side of the bed, stand and face the day anyway because I know she's going to have the sweetest voice in Heaven. Though I may not even care what her voice sounds like in Heaven. Our joy at being in the presence of God will be so consuming, the fact that my child once couldn't speak will be the faintest of memories. That's perfection I can't come close to creating in my family, and that's joy for which I'm more than willing to wait.

For now, I'll take the little glimpses God blesses me with to keep me running the race (or plodding the course). When I lie down with Lauren at night and, in the dark, she finds my face, turns it toward hers and plants a kiss on my cheek for the first time, pucker and all, I'll close my eyes and whisper, "Thank you. I can wait for the rest."

PART IV
Recommended Reading

The following is a list of books that have been most beneficial to me over the years, as I've tried to figure out Lauren while coping with autism's many repercussions. I may have forgotten one or two that I read early on. I certainly haven't included every good read here, because I haven't read everything out there. But hopefully this will give you a good broad-based start in your search for more information and support.

1. Donnellan, Anne M. and Martha O'Leary
    Movement Differences and Diversity in Autism/Mental Retardation

    Donnellan and O'Leary gave a two-day workshop I attended. Even if you've seen either of them in person, buy this book. It helped me realize the extent to which movement differences are part of Lauren's many "behaviors."

2. Gerlach, Elizabeth
    Autism Treatment Guide

    Keep this little guide on hand to explain any therapies you may hear about for autism. It's a basic, but comprehensive, guide to all the treatment options available. Gerlach stays fairly neutral while presenting the merits and drawbacks to each approach. The book has come out in an updated edition at least once, and I hope it continues to be updated on a regular basis.

3. Grandin, Temple
    Emergence, Labeled Autistic

    Though I didn't finally buy this book until later, I read many journal articles by Temple Grandin within the first weeks of Lauren's diagnosis. She's a woman with autism who has a Ph.D. and is foremost in her (unique) field of work. She opened my eyes to all the sensory issues Lauren was facing, which helped me to make major decisions about Lauren's education. Temple may be at the opposite end of the autism spectrum from my daughter, but she taught me much that is applicable to Lauren. This is her original autobiography, which includes her childhood, and has been republished. *Thinking in Pictures* is her more recent biographical work.

4. Hart, Charles
    A Parent's Guide to Autism: Answers to the Most Common Questions

This was the first book Craig and I read and it answered all our basic questions. The writer understands well the huge joy a person with autism can be. (I've heard him speak.) He grew up with a brother with autism and has a grown son with autism.

5. Lovett, Herb
    Learning to Listen: Positive Approaches and People with Difficult Behavior

This book was a wonderful quick vacation read for me. Herb Lovett's life was dedicated to helping others see what is so hard to see in people with difficult behavior—that they're people first, with the same needs and desires as all other people. It sounds obvious in the saying, but trust me that it's rare in the practice. A few years ago, I attended a day-long event with Lovett and Donna Williams, where I bought this book. At a later engagement, he and I spoke. I had written a review of this book for our local ASA newsletter. He asked for a copy of the review and I brought him one before the end of the conference. Herb Lovett died in an automobile accident within a few months of that conversation. I'm glad I took the time to get him the copy of my article, which of course was very positive. As my personal means to honor this man's life, I continue to enthusiastically recommend his work.

6.   Park, Clara Claiborne
     The Siege: The First Eight Years of an Autistic Child (With an Epilogue, Fifteen Years After)

I've read a few biographies by parents of children with autism. Some require a bit of patience getting past the self-indulgent writing style. Park's writing style is beautiful. What I love most is her description of her daughter. I've relieved myself of the responsibility of putting into words the perfection and intelligence of my daughter so subtly evident over the years. Park has done it for me.

7.   Shaw, William
     Biological Treatments for Autism and PDD

I didn't have this book when beginning medical and diet interventions for Lauren's autism. I purchased it later to try to further my understanding and to help Craig and me decide on our next step. I recommend starting with the section at the end called "Frequently Asked Questions about Dietary Intervention for the Treatment of Autism and other Developmental Disabilities" by Karyn Seroussi. These are the same (or similar) questions and answers I referred to in my "Alternative Medicine" chapter. This section offers a terrific overview, then the index can lead you to more specific explanations and supporting research on the topic you choose. (This is my advice for reading a medical book. I'm a writer, not a scientist, no matter how many years of practice I get with Lauren!)

8.   Tada, Joni Eareckson & Steven Estes
     When God Weeps: Why Our Suffering Matters to the Almighty

My experience includes many days of depression associated with the day-to-day struggles that come with autism. I imagine such days are inevitable for anyone in similar circumstances. This book is the best answer I have for you when you're too angry to speak to God or are looking for any "good" reason that this could have happened to your child and your life. Joni Eareckson Tada has been a quadriplegic for many years as the result of an accident, so I trust she knows wherefrom she speaks.

9. Williams, Donna
    Nobody Nowhere

Donna Williams is an adult with autism who was diagnosed at around twenty years old. Though I think she was higher functioning than Lauren as a child, her experiences sound in many ways more like Lauren's than Temple Grandin's. (I heard Temple speak at a dinner once. She places Donna and herself at opposite ends of a chart of the autism spectrum.) This book is tough because Donna was an abused child of poor and stupid parents and she doesn't pull any punches. (She probably can't. At the least, people with autism are honest.) Donna followed this book up with a continuing biography called *Somebody Somewhere*, but I found the first one a little more valuable, perhaps because Donna was young in the first book. Donna Williams has written more books since these two. I have *Autism: An Inside-Out Approach*. I find this to be an intense read, so I've used it as a reference tool, answering questions about Lauren's behavior by referring to the index and flipping to Donna's experience in whatever arena we're in that day.

APPENDIX A

The latest in therapy and following Lauren's progress.

In 1995, the Autism Research Institute(ARI) began Defeat Autism Now! (DAN!), a forum for researchers and practitioners to come together, compare notes about physiological treatments that have proven successful for people with autism, and to develop a protocol for treatment. This protocol addresses the unique history and symptoms of the individual and advises testing according to this specific information. There are DAN! practitioners throughout the United States and in Europe. ARI keeps an updated list by state on their website. There have been many DAN! conferences and meetings to continually update and investigate the newest in treatment options. In 2001, DAN! participants met to specifically discuss mercury detoxification, as the evidence for mercury poisoning as a cause of autism has grown rapidly within the last few years. The DAN! protocol has been regularly updated and is available from ARI in a published, manual form.

As our family's next adventure in therapy, we're going all the way. We have found a DAN! doctor. Lauren, and her history, has been examined and she will soon be undergoing testing. All of the therapies and diagnoses presented in the "Alternative Medicine, Diet and Sleep" chapter of this book played a big part in our DAN! doctor understanding what problems plague Lauren. Her successes with diet restriction and supplementation point to problems that hopefully can be solved. Rather than continuing to deny Lauren foods, we hope that we will heal the digestive problems that are making these foods intolerable to her. We are also going to pursue mercury detoxification, as a list of symptoms of mercury poisoning looks like a description of Lauren's behavior.

You may learn how Lauren is doing following the DAN! protocol by going to **www.dancingincornmeal.com**. This may be a first—being able to follow a child through a therapy without knowing the results. I have no agenda, except to present our experience with the DAN! protocol as it unfolds. (And to do all I can to heal Lauren, of course.) This will provide other families the opportunity to have unbiased information at their fingertips about one person's success or failure with the protocol. I couldn't find such information when my family was making a decision about pursuing a DAN! practitioner. However, always remember what I have said many times in this book. Each person with autism is unique. Our family's experience with the DAN! protocol may be extremely different from what another family would experience. I believe the DAN! protocol's remarkableness is its unique and thorough approach to each individual. Having said this, hopefully our family's experience will aid other families in their decision-making.

APPENDIX B

Going Gluten-Free

A t the end of the article from Dr. Beth was a web site address which contained every piece of information I needed. (The site I used was **www.autismndi.com**, which contained links to other sites where I found some of the information I put to use. Another useful site was **www.gfcfdiet.com**, which linked to the first site.) All the information on these sites is overwhelming at first, so I'll share with you what I did, in case it makes the whole process seem less intimidating.

First, I read the concise "Frequently Asked Questions" (FAQ) page of the first web site I mentioned. I printed it out, so when I forget the why's of what I'm doing, I can easily reread them.[34]

Second, I wrote down *all* the foods Lauren would currently eat. When I took her off dairy, her repertoire of foods increased significantly. (The information in the FAQ section of the web site listed explains how eliminating foods your child is intolerant of may make new foods more palatable to him or her.) Then I listed all the items that would have to be removed or replaced to go gluten-free. This made me realize that there were already a lot of gluten-free foods that Lauren would eat, and that while I was learning, she wouldn't starve.

Third, I took the list of favorite foods that she couldn't have, searched the long lists of acceptable gluten-free products and wrote down all the brands to try to replace what she would have to give up. This greatly helped in making the task seem less daunting. You see, there's really no need to keep a long list that includes acceptable alcohol beverages and salad dressings, for example, when these things are not items your child would eat anyway. You just need a short, personalized list of items you will need for your specific family.

Fourth, I made up a list of all the meals we could eat that are gluten and dairy-free (GFCF). I focused on what we could have, rather than what we couldn't have. This made it seem so doable. I add to the list as I discover how to cook an old favorite in a new way, or when the kids start eating something they never liked before. I also wrote up a list of all the snacks and drinks Lauren could have so that if she was somewhere else (she was in school at the time) the people there would know to give her these items, nothing else. I keep copies on hand, just in case we need them.

Fifth, I took a day to go shopping with my personalized list of specialty GFCF foods in hand, starting first at my regular grocery store, then at my health food store. After each item on the list, I wrote where I'd found it, or the brand I did find and where, as I found some new products that are GFCF. When I arrived home, I made a grocery list with two columns. I wrote the name of a store at the head of each column, then listed underneath the foods we would have to buy there. (I have since added a third and fourth column, as I'm finding my favorite products on some web sites and I just have them shipped.)

Lastly, I photocopied the list of no-no ingredients that was on one of the web sites I mentioned earlier. (Gluten and casein are rarely listed clearly on ingredient labels.) I carry this with me at all times so if I stop for groceries and can't find my usual brand, I can look at another brand's list of ingredients. You'll find that gluten can be hidden in the ingredient "natural flavors," which seems to be in everything. I've actually called the 800 number on the label of a product on my cell phone from the grocery store. Most companies are very good at quickly telling you whether their product has gluten in it, as gluten is very harmful to people with the condition called celiac disease.

Our whole family eats gluten and casein-free as Lauren doesn't understand that these things hurt her, so it would be cruel to eat them in front of her. We do make exceptions for some foods that Lauren never showed any interest in anyway, such as tortillas and hot dog rolls. If we want to cheat, we wait until Lauren is in bed, then have ice cream or something we miss. At first, Bryn lost weight rapidly and was looking emaciated, so I bought her a few "glutenful" snack foods that she kept in a container in a closet. She asked permission to eat them, then went into the office/homeschool room, locked the door and enjoyed her snack with a good book. But even Bryn started feeling better after getting gluten (or the wheat or yeast component) out of her system. She used to get a stomach ache after eating many bread products, but she never gets them anymore. She's now fallen in love with some gluten-free snacks we've found, so we don't have the glutenful stash anymore. Though, every now and then she does hide out to have PB&J or turkey on good ol' white bread, which we occasionally "hide" in the fridge by keeping it in a plastic grocery bag.

In an e-mail exchange, one mom once wrote that even though she thought her son might benefit from going gluten-free she didn't think she could implement the diet because it would be too difficult on the other family members. I thought a lot about this before responding. When I did respond (including all the tips you just read here), I also asked the mom to imagine that the allergy was to something more obvious, such as ant bites. Wouldn't the whole family be extra cautious not to let an ant get past them and into their home? Wouldn't the other children be diligent, even sacrificial if necessary, to protect the health, and possibly the life, of their brother? If not, then the family has bigger problems than gluten getting into the child with autism.

About the Author

Nannette Beyea Silvernail is a graduate of Russell Sage College in Troy, New York with a B.A. in English. Her poetry, articles and essays have been published in multiple minor publications over the years. *Dancing in Cornmeal* is her first full-length book.

Ms. Silvernail has been involved with her local Autism Society of America chapter as secretary, newsletter editor and member of the Board of Directors. She has been homeschooling her two daughters since their preschool years and has taught children with autism in a private school setting.

When Ms. Silvernail is not writing, she continues in her full-time career as mom and homeschool teacher/therapist. She lives in Georgia with her husband, two daughters and four cats.

Endnotes

1. I'll explain stimming thoroughly in the chapter entitled "Drop the Stimmy…"

2. Urinary Tract Infection

3. Don't worry if too much new information was just thrown at you in this paragraph. I'll discuss these things in more detail in later chapters. I've included so much in this paragraph to convey how very complicated life with Lauren has become.

4. Tests may be performed to rule out other possible diagnoses or underlying problems.

5. Consult the *Diagnostic and Statistical Manual* (currently the *DSM-IV*) of the American Psychiatric Association (APA) for an accurate listing of APA accepted diagnostic criteria.

6. I've also heard professionals say that PDD stands for Pervasive Developmental Dysfunction and Pervasive Developmental Disability. I mention this here because I think the word "delay" is inaccurate and misleading in describing autism.

7. Donna Williams was diagnosed with autism as an adult and has written at least four books based on her experience.

8. Magnetic Resonance Imaging

9. "Test offers new clues on causes of autism," *The Democrat and Chronicle*, 4 May 2000, p. 7A

10. See Appendix A at the end of this book for information about treatment which addresses mercury toxicity and other causal factors mentioned in this chapter.

11. Yes, I mean all milestones listed in the average baby book that covers the years right up until Kindergarten. Lauren had met all milestones expected during her first year. It wasn't until after her first year (and after many scheduled immunizations) that her loss of old skills and lack of new ones began to slowly become apparent.

12. In later chapters, I tell how Lauren's rate of ear infection dropped significantly once she began receiving chiropractic care.

13. Untreated ear infections can, in extreme cases, lead to mastoiditis or meningitis, both of which are serious conditions. Therefore, it's very important to have a trusted practitioner monitor your child's ears until the infection is gone.

14. Lauren doesn't just come into skin contact with pool water; she doesn't understand not to drink it. She becomes sick immediately after swimming. Then she's a sensory mess with atrocious behavior for two weeks afterward, apparently until the chemicals have cleared her system. I mention this in the next chapter, as well.

15. Stimming is the act of exhibiting self-stimulating behavior, such as rocking or hand-flapping. The chapter in this book entitled "Drop the Stimmy…" is a thorough discussion (and attempt at explanation) of such behavior.

16. IEP stands for Individualized Educational Plan, which is the document listing the goals and methods of a child's educational program. The purpose of an IEP meeting is to write or improve an IEP so that it best meets the needs of the specific child. The IEP is updated in such a meeting at least once a year. Whenever change in a program's effectiveness is suspected, a parent or teacher may call for additional IEP meetings.

17. I've also heard this called *reverse chaining*.

18. Some of the therapies mentioned in this chapter are becoming generally accepted within the autism community and should not necessarily be labeled "alternative." However, many traditional medical doctors do not keep up with autism research or are simply skeptical of approaches they didn't encounter in medical school. These doctors would likely categorize some of these approaches as alternative. Also, each of the approaches my family has taken were logical steps, at the time, for pursuing tangible reasons for Lauren's problems. Each family's course will be different because each child and family is unique. See Appendix A at the end of this book for related, very important information.

19. Lauren had a parasite named cryptosporidium in her digestive tract. These parasites are found in some water supplies, but they rarely survive in healthy humans. They thrive in the crevices (crypts) that are symptomatic of an unhealthy digestive tract.

20. Go to the website of the Autism Research Institute (ARI) to find the research history behind the creation of these supplements. B6/Magnesium and DMG are both nutritional supplements about which ARI founder Bernard Rimland has compiled impressive statistics.

21. The doctor said it must be an allergic reaction to something she ate. (She hadn't recently eaten anything unusual.) He recommended putting Vaseline or some other lip protection on the lips to help them stay moist so they could heal. Instead, I ground up a chewable acidophilus (pro-biotic) tablet so that it was chalk-like. When she fell asleep at night, I used a cotton ball to dab as much of the powdery substance as possible all over her lips. She looked much better by morning and was completely healed the morning after a second night's treatment. So much for protecting the lips with moisture.

22. See Appendix A at the end of this book for more information about our continuing adventures with "alternative" therapies, as well as information about following these adventures on our website.

23. Perseveration is a word used in the field of disabilities to describe persistent, often obsessive, preoccupation with one topic or activity. Perseverative talking (or perseverative speech) describes a person's verbal perseveration.

24. Dr. Sayer's character is based on Dr. Oliver Sacks, who wrote the book, *Awakenings*. I recommend this and all of Oliver Sacks's writings.

25. Donna Williams is the author with autism I mentioned in an earlier chapter called "The Four Questions" under the subtitle, "What is Autism?"

26. "Art" and "Birds" may not be the best examples of this experiment, but they were really Bryn and Craig's responses when I asked while writing this chapter, and I promised myself I would use whatever they said. Perhaps the words "vacation" or "shopping" would provide more obvious material, but I'm glad neither said one of those, or my list would be as long as this whole book!

27. Phrenologists were "scientists" in the 1800's who determined a person's intelligence by the size and shape of the skull. Of course, most men's skulls are larger than women's and all phrenologists were men.

28. Carole Swick is an autism consultant in private practice specializing in behavioral management.

29. Parish School of Religion (Sunday School)

30. "I Want to Know You" was written by Andy Park and recorded by SonicFlood.

31. Yes, this is the same story told (for a different purpose) in the chapter entitled "School."

32. This may be an issue in the autism community only because the word "autistic" is sometimes used as a noun instead of an adjective. To understand the problem with this, consider the insensitivity of saying "the retard" or "the black" instead of saying "the retarded child" or "the black man."

33. In the chapter called "The Four Questions" under "What is Autism?" I discuss the inherent problems to a diagnostic system that lumps speaking and non-speaking children of varying ages under a vague diagnosis of Pervasive Developmental Delay (PDD). Non-duplicable miracle cures are one of those problems.

34. This FAQ information is also available in William Shaw's book, *Biological Treatments for Autism and PDD*. For further explanation, see the Recommended Reading section of this book.

0-595-22833-X